Degrees of Difference

By the same author

Class and Skill, Changing Divisions of Knowledge and Labour, Cassell 1993.

Young People Leaving Home, with 86 young people in Kirk-caldy, Liverpool, Sheffield and Swindon and a statistical afterword by Sheena Ashford, Cassell 1991.

Training for the Future, the rise and fall of the Manpower Services Commission, with Mark Corney, Cassell 1990.

Vocational Education and Training, in Education Matters series (general editor, Ted Wragg), Cassell 1990.

From School to YTS, Education and Training in England and Wales 1944–1987, Open University Press 1988.

Falling Apart, The coming crisis of Conservative education, with Ken Jones et al., the Tufnell Press 1992.

Training Turns to Enterprise, Vocational Education in the Marketplace, the Tufnell Press 1990.

Degrees of Difference

Higher Education in the 1990s

PATRICK AINLEY

Lawrence & Wishart
LONDON

Lawrence & Wishart Limited
144a Old South Lambeth Road
London SW8 1XX

First Published 1994 by Lawrence & Wishart
© Patrick Ainley 1994

ISBN 0–85315–804–5

Typeset in Baskerville by Lucy Morton
71 Effingham Road, London SE12
Printed and bound by Biddles Ltd,
Guildford and King's Lynn

Three hours to answer four questions.
Three years to answer none.

'Lines on a Cambridge Tripos Paper',
Johanne Peter (aka Fredddy Fritz) 1971

Contents

Acknowledgements

This book turned out to be harder and to take longer to write than any of my other efforts in recent years. At first I thought I could write it in a short time, students being easy people to interview – for the most part they are articulate and quick to latch on to what you want from them. I must therefore thank all the students interviewed for this study. I am sorry they have had so long to wait for the book but I hope they will find something of themselves in here, even if their lively interviews and conversations have become somewhat buried in the other perspectives that have come to inform the book. At first I thought that they might feature more prominently, indeed that it might even be possible to write the book entirely in their own words, as a sort of continuous collective stream of consciousness reflecting upon their experiences. All that remains of this idea is the complete transcriptions of their interviews which, on disc and cleaned of any personally identifying characteristics, are available on application to the author for students to use as practice in the analysis of qualitative data. Such exercises are increasingly rare nowadays in social sciences being pushed by new technology towards purely quantitative statistical analyses. Hopefully students will find the complete interviews interesting in their own right, as reflecting the opinions and experiences of people in a similar situation to their own if a few years earlier, and not just as a check upon the veracity of the interpretation put upon them in this book. The idea of such an exercise was suggested to me – to make another acknowledgement – by Claire Wallace of the European University.

The complexity of the issues that the interviews with the students raised and the effort to express them simply without simplification soon put paid to my first simplistic ideas for the book and as time passed it expanded into a series of interviews also with academic staff. It would be invidious to name them all here but I am grateful to them above all for their being willing to put in the hands of a stranger what one of them called, 'the short-handing of a lifetime's experience'. To Professor Arnold Goldman and Doctor Phil Brown who made the study possible in the first place I am particularly indebted. Also to Dr. Derek Robbins, whose life's work in making the writings of the great French sociologist of education, Pierre Bourdieu, accessible to English readers has been a source of constant inspiration. The 'We' in the text is not a royal prerogative of the author but refers to ideas that I felt Derek and I developed in common together in the course of our collaboration.

Professor Richard Norman and David Morgan of Kent University, Professor Stewart Ranson of Birmingham and Dr. Ron Barnet of the London University Institute of Education's Centre for Higher Education Studies, Dr. Sheena Ashford at Warwick and Paul Frew, who took time off from writing his remarkable hyperpoetry, all kindly read bits of the manuscript at various stages or at least talked to me about it and gave me carefully considered and constructive comments, not all of which were taken but all of which were well meant. I am indebted too to Dr. Jenny Corbett, Mike Laycock and Barry Richards at East London University and to Professor Tyrrell Burgess, who is a walking institution in his own right. My thanks also to Glen Rikowski for showing me the relevance of Nietzsche's philosophy to pedagogy today and to Colin Waugh's articles in NATFHE's *General Educator* for his clear exposition of Marx's idea of polytechnic education. I enjoyed many a long conversation with John Greer of the University Careers Service and Selina Springbett. I must also thank John Offord and his colleagues at the National Union of Students' research department, as well as Alan Marr for the account of his research into the awarding of fine art degrees retailed in Chapter three. Also, Rupert Brown of the AUT for his survey of university staff. Despite her enthusiasm for postmodernism, I valued too my publisher, Sally Davison's, careful attention to the text. To all of the above and to Maureen Nunn, Elizabeth Edwards, Christine Hooper, Lewis Elton, Jane Austick, Frank Burnet, Alan Bunch, Beatrice Shire and others involved in the Enterprise Initiative at Kent University also many thanks for their forbearance and help. In this last but not least regard – to Beulah and Adam for their usual but unusual patience.

Introduction

This book is written primarily for and about students of the new further, higher and adult education system. To students and teachers of education, sociology, cultural studies and cognate subjects it will be a part of their subject of study and one, moreover, related to their own experience in education. However, we hope that its readership will not be confined to specialists, for the present rapid changes in further, higher and adult education are of wider concern. The book is therefore intended to put what must often be confusing student experiences in a wider context and to make understandable to them and to other readers the changes that have occurred, as well as the new measures that are proposed.

So the book is also for anyone who is interested and perhaps worried about what is happening to education at all levels in our rapidly changing society. For the present transformation in what is now a linked system of further, higher and adult education affects not only the schools which prepare students for entry to the range of colleges and universities. It also affects adults, in and out of formal education and training, in work and out, who are today also entering higher education in greater numbers than ever before. Yet it is remarkable that these huge changes have gone largely unnoticed and have not been discussed outside the specialist educational press, and even there only in that section of it devoted to higher education. It is time to make them comprehensible to as wide an audience as possible and so open them up for wider debate.

We have tried therefore to make the book as accessible as possible. Especially as much of the internal debate that does go on in higher education is carried out at a high level of obscurity, often in its own self-referring jargon of 'fitness for purpose', 'quality' and 'higher cognitive skills' – terms which, if they mean anything, do so only to a small number of higher education auditors, managers and researchers. Our description by contrast is in the

simplest possible terms but hopefully without simplifying the issues. It is not an academic approach although it attempts to make
plain certain academic concepts. References have therefore been
relegated to what is only a brief bibliography.

Students themselves are the most important people to involve
in this discussion about the present shape and future direction of
the further and higher education system. They, along with the
people who teach them and staff the colleges and universities, are
under growing pressure. What are they to make of the bewildering
array of courses and option choices that often face them, along
with new methods of learning and assessment? What do these
mean not only for their own future, happiness and interests but
for other students in the system, for the economy for which their
learning may or may not be preparing them and for the culture
and civilisation of which higher education is a part?

It is often as much as most students can do to keep up with the
reading that is required of them to meet tight schedules, crammed
with new programmes of learning and experience, before they
can even begin to think about such wider questions. They rarely
have time to reflect formally upon the purposes of their study and
whether it is helping them to get what they want out of it; let
alone, what all the changes that are happening around them mean
for the future of society and the world. These are the questions
that are addressed in this book.

It aims to open up to students the wider picture of which their
own studies and their particular college or university is a part. It
does not present any easy answers to the complicated questions
that are raised, although we have our own recommendations at
the end of the book for the general direction that further, higher,
adult and, indeed, schools education should take. These are offered
as a contribution to the continuing debate about the direction
and purposes of education and training, of learning and teaching,
which we hope the book will help to stimulate and inform.

We have not written down to our readers by attempting to
simplify the issues involved. The cultural, economic, social and
historical context of educational change is indeed complex. We
can only begin to draw together the themes for its discussion in
the introduction. The reader may begin here or leave such general
considerations for later, preferring to plunge into the middle of
things by starting with the student interviews in chapter two.

This second chapter sets the scene by examining two contrasted higher education institutions. They are chosen as representative of opposite ends of the academic and social hierarchy that is emerging in higher education. We use students' own words to discover what higher education today is like as they experience and understand it in two very different parts of the new university system. The quotations used are excerpted from interviews undertaken in 1991 with selected samples of final year students at the two universities.

To get an idea of where the new and evolving system is going we then use interviews with a smaller sample of their lecturers and professors collected a year later. These enable us to identify the emerging features of the new system and to discuss them in the framework of opposed directions that education and society could take as it enters the third millennium. We present an outline of the dominant tendencies and then argue for what we call, following the pioneering work of Pierre Bourdieu, a rational pedagogy.

Rational pedagogy would combine learning and teaching, in whatever subject or combination of subjects, with an explanation of its aims and methods with reference to the wider social processes of which it forms a part. The students thus come to understand not only their own subject of study but also themselves and their situation. This leads to the independent thought and study, the discovery and creation, that we believe should be a part of learning for all students at all levels of education. For this to take place as a matter of course, and not just exceptionally or occasionally, requires a democratic reconstruction of the entire society that will go far beyond educational institutions, but of which education and training will form a vital part.

For independent thought and action is also necessary for the whole of society if people are to take the future in their own hands. Unthinking adherence to old ideas, habitual reflexes and traditional customs have led to the present economic, social and political impasse which threatens cultural and ecological degradation if not catastrophe in the near future. New discovery and creation is urgently required for humanity's survival; and the new higher education should be one place to nurture it. We hope that this book is a small contribution to the revaluation of human purposes that is urgently needed if in the future humanity is to exercise its unique capacity of learning from past experience to avoid the foreseeable consequences of its present actions.

Mass Higher Education

Two types of education

Learning to live

What makes human beings different from other animals is their ability to learn from the past to alter their behaviour in the future.

This unique potential is present to only a limited extent in nature. Even though animals can acquire the ability or be trained to perform complicated routines, it is rare that they can pass on more than a small part of these acquired characteristics to future generations. For most animals such learning is exceptional rather than the rule. Apart from a few behaviours like birdsong (possibly), animal ability to learn from and to teach each other is largely restricted to some of the other primates. This is because the other animals lack a symbolic consciousness which can be expressed in the symbols of language proper. Instead, animal behaviour is predominantly predetermined by inherited instincts. It is therefore only by genetic adaptations that behaviour can be altered and this is an extremely lengthy process of evolution.

By contrast, human learning communicated by culture and embodied in manufactured objects – those twin creations of the two tools of language and technology – relearns and represents to each successive generation the whole expanding body of human knowledge about the universe we inhabit and our purposes in it. The succession of the generations which makes this necessary also makes possible the innovations that open the door to new knowledge and which come, generally speaking, from the new minds of each generation. Humanity can thus justifiably be described as the learning species. In this sense the English artist, craftsman and socialist, William Morris, was right to say that 'We learn to live and live to learn'.

The future of our species now depends more than ever on the speed with which we can learn and what we now take to be worth learning. For human history has reached a point when, unless human survival is consciously taken as the prime purpose of social endeavour, we may not survive as a species for very much longer, certainly not for another millennium. The alterations which we have made in the environment that sustains us are causing unpredictable but possibly catastrophic climatic and other changes in the biosphere. Already successively critical thresholds are being crossed and we have to ask ourselves whether it is the ultimate purpose of individuals and the societies they make up to produce and consume more and more commodities at the cost of further degrading the planetary ecology and impoverishing the mass of humanity, or whether the finality of human being is not to be found in the survival of our species and the planetary ecology which sustains it.

In this sense we can no longer live by the Utopian goals that accompanied the transition to a modern, industrial economy. They will have to be replaced by the recognition of what is necessary for human survival. Neither the free market Utopia of Adam Smith in which the endless production of commodities could supposedly satisfy all individual demands, nor the collective Utopia of Karl Marx, that also sought to pass from necessity to freedom upon the basis of the production of a superfluity of commodities, were open to the necessity of integrating society with the ecology that sustains it. So, as survival replaces Utopia, a shift in perspective is required towards a view of the world that determines the knowledge now useful for the survival of our species.

What is useful knowledge?

What was considered socially useful knowledge at different times and in different places always came from three main sources. These are, firstly, social experience – either directly by participation in society or, for the most part, indirectly from records of times past and the histories of other cultures; secondly, from the lessons learnt from refining and developing tools and machinery to increase production with greater efficiency and less laborious effort; and, lastly, from scientific experiment, especially once agreed procedures had been reached amongst what became a world scientific community for validating experimental results by commonly accepted criteria.

Really useful knowledge was until modern times directly vocational. It was used by those who acquired it in the productive work that they undertook for their own and society's direct benefit. However, even before the neolithic revolution introduced settled agriculture and herding, when it is probable that mature individuals were familiar with all the culture, technology and 'science' of their time, there was a division of labour and hence of knowledge. It was based upon age and gender. In early tribal societies it seems that mental work in handing down the traditions of the tribe and the technical expertise acquired during a lifetime was the specialised function of the old whose wisdom was universally revered. Through age-grading an individual acquired in turn and by initiation all the skills shared by their gender in the collectivity as a whole.

It was only with the development of technology allowing for the production of a surplus sufficient to feed some members of society who did not have to work to produce it that the mental work of organising the efforts of others emerged as a life-long and specialised occupation in its own right. At first the chiefs who directed the efforts of societies to greater effect usually took over command from a council of elders only in emergency situations, as in the native American institution of war-chiefs. Eventually though, chiefs came to maintain their privileged position with an armed bodyguard of their relatives. Historical reconstruction suggests that in most cases, for someone not to have to spend their life on hard labour was regarded as such a remarkable phenomenon by the working majority that the first rulers were everywhere accorded the status of god-kings who were literally not of this earth.

These guardians of society were held to possess and thought themselves in possession of an other worldly and secret knowledge communicated to them by exclusive and mysterious rituals. Even though their position more often than not soon became hereditary, elevation to their ranks depended primarily upon proficiency in a series of trials in the form essentially of question and answer. Such riddles, which so many archaic societies jealously preserved, presented generalised knowledge about structures rather than facts. They made accessible through the manipulation of symbolic objects, with appropriate actions, images, words and music, the general, theoretical laws which enabled initiates to make sense of and generalise their experience and hence introduced them to a way of thinking different from that of the subjects on whose behalf they made important decisions. This was what Aristotle, writing about tribal scieties in the process of forming city-states, called 'the knowledge necessary to rule'. It was not a knowledge of everything but of the rules by which the totality of known facts could be acquired and ordered.

It was a form of knowledge that, as it was elaborated by specialist shamen, priests and philosophers, tended to become increasingly reflexive and reflective, knowing also the grounds for its own knowing and able to justify them against rival systems of interpretation, but open also to more or less logical correction in the face of new evidence and argument. It was therefore, among other things, a form of argument that could win assent other than by the use of force. Systems of generalised knowledge could thus move towards higher levels of containment and explanation as the quantity of available information grew. They could also become open to higher levels of determination in terms of the justifications they were able to give of human and natural events, the point of their closure being their mark as ideologies expressing the particular world views of dominant tribes or nations and the ruling castes or classes within them.

For the ancient civilisations of India, China and elsewhere, as in the West, this generalised knowledge was shared less and less by the majority over whom the emerging ruling castes and classes exercised their authority. The knowledge of the labouring majority was more and more confined to the vocational information necessary for them to complete their productive work. Vocational information can therefore be said to be 'closed' at a lower level than generalised knowledge and to be contained or encompassed by it.

The method of induction into this generalised and privileged level of thought by means of question and answer was extended into a prolonged conversation. It became a type of apprenticeship by which the mysteries of abstract or generalised knowledge were handed down the generations of the Guardians who had to be educated to rule. For the West, this was the origin and the ideal of the Platonic Academy that has exercised such a long-lasting influence upon European university education.

Indeed, if one visits a traditional university today, what is going on in most of the lecture and seminar rooms, let alone in the informal meetings of students on and off campus, is talking – not doing. The range of activities is generally very narrow: lectures in which one person talks to many, seminars or 'workshops' in which the numbers are reduced – in the case of tutorials to one to one. Only in the laboratories and workshops, the studios and theatres of the applied sciences and arts, is this not the case. In the mainstream, even the one-way communication of traditional lectures finds its point in what students together make of them afterwards. The danger is of course that so much verbiage becomes empty of content and so deprived of meaning that it is alienated from reality, and alienating to 'uneducated' people, who are more or less confined to limited occupation information – but that often can be half the object of the exercise!

Such abstract, generalised knowledge was for long deliberately kept distinct from the vocational information individuals required to participate directly in the processes of production. However, as even the most abstract knowledge derived ultimately from practical experience – even if people thought that such 'truths' came to them from some sort of other worldly inspiration – there remained the ideal, reanimated at various times – as for example by some artists in the European Renaissance, of combining theory and practice in the form of what became known as polytechnic education.

Polytechnic education

The phrase 'polytechnic education', meaning an education derived from practical work rather than abstracted from speculation, exercised such a predominant influence over socialist educators both within and outwith the former Soviet Union, yet it derives curiously from a mistranslation. Karl Marx had used the English phrase 'technological training' to indicate the type of education system he envisioned in the socialist future. This was translated into German in words which if literally turned back into English would mean 'polytechnic education' and this doubtful translation stuck in the systems of education erected in the former-socialist countries.

Even though the theoretical basis for this vast and ultimately unsuccessful social experiment was no more than a few sentences written at different times by Marx and his collaborator Engels, the little that the founders of 'scientific socialism' wrote on the subject of education shows profound philosophical differences with other approaches to pedagogy. By insisting that 'social being determines consciousness', rather than that ideas are innate in the mind or come to people through more or less divine inspiration, Marx indicated that how you think depends on how you have been brought up. Education should not therefore rely upon the handing down of received authority – or the dogma that replaced thought as 'actually existing socialism' degenerated into state capitalism in the former Soviet Union. Learning should, according to Marx, instead be a collective endeavour, carried out jointly by teachers and taught, tackling real-life problems and reflecting upon the results.

Moreover, such an education could not only, or even mainly, be provided by schools and colleges. For Marx's polytechnic ideal of education drew upon the earlier Chartist tradition of 'really useful knowledge' with which English workers at the beginning of the nineteenth century sought to understand for themselves the new-born industrial society, and how to better their place in it. For the Chartists, their education in really useful knowledge occurred outside formal institutions of learning and was aimed as much at adults as at younger people. It did not aim to be purely contemplative of reality regarded objectively, as was claimed by the 'gentlemanly', humanist or liberal tradition of education inherited by the English ruling class from the Ancients and the church. Instead, it sought to supersede this traditional form of knowledge, which it recognised as an ideology, by solving practical problems, actively changing the reality of which it recognised itself as a part.

Marx's polytechnic ideal combined this Chartist self-reliance in mutual study and teaching with the other main tradition of socialist education in Britain at that time which was exemplified by the progressive factory owner, Robert Owen. During the first half of the nineteenth century, he had established schools for the children working with their parents in his factory community at New Lanark in Scotland. These schools were seen by Marx as 'the germ of the education of the future'. However, Marx also thought that the paternalistic management of Owen's factory schooling forgot that 'the educators must themselves be educated'. In other words, the teachers, brought up in the old world, had as much to learn as those they taught. Teaching was therefore a collective, two-way process in which people essentially had to educate themselves, if for no other reason than that no one can learn for you. In Marx's conception, such an education therefore tended to do away with the distinction between teachers and taught, in which (classically) the clever sage instructs the ignorant fool, in favour of a mutual endeavour to learn together more than they already knew.

For the question of who produces knowledge and for what purpose was a central issue for Marx as much as it had been for his Chartist predecessors. Since the point of popular knowledge was not merely to understand but to change the world for their own benefit as a class at the expense of their masters, working people could not rely passively upon the answers being handed down to them by the existing authorities. Instead, really useful knowledge had to be actively discovered in a process of collective self-realisation and transformation.

To the early socialist and communist parties, Marx's axiom of combining education with productive labour was a means to this end. It did not seek to develop technical expertise for particular posts, nor familiarity with the so-called 'personal and transferable skills' required in many different occupations, so that individuals could better fit into the existing division of labour in society, as vocational education does today. Rather, it sought to overcome that division and especially the division between manual and mental labour that was so fundamental to the nineteenth century factory system and its subsequent development into 'Fordist' methods of mass production. In factories like Henry Ford's pioneering River Rouge plant at Detroit, so-called 'scientific management' used work study to subdivide the repetitive tasks of assembly-line production so that they could be organised and controlled from the office by managers. This removed, in the words of the pioneer of this approach, Frederick Taylor, the necessity for workers to think at all about what they were doing.

Instead of this divisive approach, the idea of a polytechnic education, as developed by Marx's followers in the first socialist and communist parties, was to overcome such separation of one group of workers from another. It aimed too at overcoming the exclusiveness of the mainly male craft unions which had formed by the end of the nineteenth century. By linking the technical with the general and political, workers at whatever level would come to see their place in the overall division of labour and organisation of society. Instead of as individuals, they would come to see themselves as a class and then, in Morris's words again, 'to perceive that instead of a class they ought to be society'. This original polytechnic education thus sought to build from the particular to the general, from the concrete to the abstract rather than vice versa. In the process it would develop the same generalised knowledge necessary to rule as that exercised by the old ruling class from whom it intended to take power.

As the Italian communist, Antonio Gramsci, put it in the early years of the twentieth century, 'Starting off from this original cell, the factory seen as a unit, as an act that creates a particular product, the worker proceeds to the comprehension of ever vaster units... At this point workers become producers, for they have acquired an awareness of their role in the process of production, at all its levels, from the workshop to the nation and the world.' Thus producers could educate themselves to see what was necessary for society to benefit all its members. In particular, for its own reproduction and future survival, as well as for the more equitable distribution of its products, society and the production that sustains it had to be democratically controlled by the producers themselves.

This is a very different conception of 'education for work' from the vocational preparation about which we hear so much today and which assumes that any connection between education and employment stimulates learning because it helps the individual to get a job in competition with the next person.

The polytechnics

Something of the early socialist ideal of a polytechnic education resurfaced in somewhat attenuated form with the founding of the polytechnics in England and Wales (Central Institutions in Scotland). It was Anthony Crosland, the 1964 Labour government's Education Minister, who instituted the 'binary line' between the new polytechnics that he proposed and the already existing and new universities. The university sector also included the Colleges of Arts and Technology, set up in 1956 and then elevated to the status of technical universities. Even though Crosland said that he 'did not want any rigid dividing line between the different sectors – quite the contrary', his decision institutionally polarised higher educational values and goals. It generated and sustained – in this sector of education as elsewhere – a simplified opposition between academicism and vocationalism, education and training, generalised knowledge and vocational competence.

Despite this, many of those involved in setting up the new polytechnics advocated 'higher education for all'. This would for the first time give opportunities for 'careers for all', instead of interesting, varied and progressive careers for a few and dull, repetitive and dead-end 'jobs' for the many. Seen as 'the people's universities' (in Sidney Webb's phrase) by some of their idealistic founders, the polytechnics aimed to pioneer what they called a liberal vocationalism that paralleled contemporary developments in comprehensive and community schools. Like the comprehensive schools that began to spread across the majority of local education authorities from 1965 on, the polytechnics aimed to make available for students studying locally 'equal opportunities' to qualify for occupations on equal terms with those educated selectively. Thus, one of their founders, Eric Robinson, saw the new institutions creating 'a bridgehead' for a 'comprehensive system of education for adults', replacing 'the concept of the boarding school university by that of the urban community university'. Nevertheless, he admitted, 'The British image of a polytechnic remains that of an educational soup kitchen for the poor'.

Whether that image will be changed by the 1992 changing of the names of former polytechnics to universities is one of the issues that we explore in this comparison of higher education in the Home Counties and inner city. Before reviewing in chapters two, three and four the experiences of students and then staff in two contrasted higher education institutions however, we trace in the remainder of this chapter the recent history of the two types of education that co-exist in Britain: the Western humanist or liberal ideal of academic higher education whose origins are in the ancient Greek and medieval worlds, and its opposition by a concept of polytechnic education. The latter arose out of the industrial revolution and involved practical learning from work to rise to the same abstract or general level of knowledge and of knowledge about knowledge.

This original ideal of polytechnic practical education, as has been said, aimed to use work, not in the manner of today's vocational education, as a preparation for employment, but as a pedagogical and philosophical principal. It aspired to derive general knowledge of how natural and social systems work from their particular applications. It is thus open to further expansion and does not confine students to closed knowledge about specific

occupational competencies as today's vocational education tends
to do.

This implies a particular view of where ideas – human repre-
sentations of reality – come from: from reality itself and not just
from book learning, from abstract contemplation or from the
divine inspiration of 'genius'. Instead, practical learning presents
scholarship, artistic creation and scientific research as linked
together for a purpose, not to be studied or discovered for their
own sake. However, this purpose is not limited to educating individuals for their future employment, or to producing knowledge
useful only for contributing towards the manufacture of more
commodities for sale at a profit in competition with rival
companies or 'competitor nations' – nor indeed to amassing the
detailed and subdivided specialisms of academic expertise.

The polytechnic ideal of knowledge for a practical purpose was
embodied in the original socialist ideal and in its 1960s social
democratic version. The new polytechnics were intended by the
Labour government to play a part in national manpower planning
for a regenerated economy. They were directly vocational, while
the liberal humanism of the traditional universities, pursuing
knowledge for its own sake, contributed only indirectly and, as it
were, incidentally to the economy.

For students, vocational study at polytechnics aimed to reach
the same level of generalised knowledge and higher cognitive skills
as traditional university study, but by direct application to the
world of work. This compared with the traditional liberal humanist approach to learning which was ostensibly for the sake of self-
development but actually helped students to get better jobs.
Polytechnics therefore answered more directly the question deeply
rooted in the consciousness of many students about the purpose
of their education. However, nowadays the contradiction of preparing for work that may not exist at the end of the course is
more clearly apparent to students and their teachers than ever
before, as education expands in a recession. For what students
have not, at some time, been dissatisfied with the idea that the
purpose of their study is to gain entry to an occupation that can
very often no longer be guaranteed, or that is restricted to only
a very limited exercise of the capabilities and intelligence that
they may have begun to develop during their higher education?

The question we ask in this book is whether the new further,
higher and adult education that is developing in Britain today will

contribute towards, or merely hinder, the development of new knowledge, and a collective intelligence to meet the uncertain future now faced by individuals, society and the world. The social context in which the wide-ranging changes are being introduced demands examination however, and it is to this that we now turn.

The expansion of higher education in a recession

Education and politics

In the 1992 general election the government's target for growth in higher education, to cater for one third of 18–21 year olds by the year 2000, was accepted by all parties. In Scotland indeed, this target had already been met, so that country aims for half of all its 17–21 year olds in HE by that date. Attempts by the colleges and universities during the election campaign to lobby for extra funds to finance this expansion without loss of quality were largely ignored. Higher education (at 18+) and indeed further education (at 16+) were no more an election issue than adult education – although schools (but not nursery) education was.

From its origins in an elite system of medieval Oxbridge colleges and Victorian Civic universities attended before the second world war by only 3 per cent of the population, mainly young men, higher education had grown to 7.2 per cent of the age range by 1962/3. Then, under the twin impetus of the post-war baby boom growing up into a teeny boom, coupled with the electoral demands of a broadening middle class seeking professional occupations for its children in the burgeoning bureaucracies of the Welfare State, a phase of expansion was recommended by the Conservative-sponsored Robbins Report of 1963. This led to the foundation of new universities, alongside the promotion of some technical colleges to independent university status. Robbins established the principle that 'courses of higher education should be available for all those who are qualified by ability and attainment to pursue them and who wish to do so'.

It is important to note that this often quoted Robbins principle (though it should be defended against its erosion by payment for higher education through loans or top-up fees) did not establish the universal right to attend college. Because entry was still through 'qualification by ability and attainment', Robbins simply moved selection up the age range, just as it was being phased out of state schools by the piecemeal introduction of comprehensives from 1965 on. The age of selection thus rose from 11+, to 14+ and later, with the introduction of GCSEs, to 16+. The acceptance of Robbins's recommendations by the 1964 Labour government led to a pattern of transition for growing numbers of middle-class youth, female as well as male, moving from school to work, and from home to living away, via three or four years of residential HE.

The growth of the universities was supplemented after 1965 when Anthony Crosland announced an expansion of the colleges and polytechnics under the control of local education authorities. This 'binary policy' was supposed to benefit local students following more vocational and less academic courses, related to their local labour markets. Together with the Open University (founded in 1969), it brought the percentage of full- and part-time students to 12.7 per cent of the age group by the end of the 1970s, after which a short period of cut-backs followed. With the partial, if only temporary, recovery of the economy, growth resumed. The expansion in numbers of students was accelerated by the Conservative government's sudden adoption in 1987 of the North American model of mass higher education (see below), so that by 1990 the age participation ratio (of home students under 21 compared to the total population of that age) topped 20 per cent for the first time in the UK as a whole. In polytechnics and colleges of higher education the numbers doubled from 1985, so that by 1991, also for the first time, more than half of all full-time first degree students were in polytechnics or colleges rather than universities. The number of part-time students also rose rapidly, especially in the polytechnics and colleges.

There were now more than a million full- and part-time, home and overseas higher education students, in a ratio of three to two men to women overall (excluding nurses). There were 1,268,000 in the academic year 1990/91. Half of the new student body are outside the stereotypical 18–21 age range and many live at home rather than move away to study. Approximately 13 per cent of them are postgraduates, whose numbers increased by 65 per cent throughout the 1980s, particularly on one-year taught Masters courses as a requirement for three-year Doctoral studies. This would seem to anticipate the formation of US-style graduate schools. Numbers of postgraduate students are projected to rise further even though there are not sufficient finances due to a squeeze of government research funding. At this level of study, there is also an effort to reduce support for the arts and social sciences and to direct postgraduate students towards science and technology.

This increase in numbers has been achieved despite an increase in fees (recoverable by the universities and colleges from public funds) and the introduction of loans to pay for student grants. By 1991 the average student was leaving full-time higher education £2,000 in debt, according to a survey by a prominent High Street bank. With its 1993 budget the government reneged on previous promises to freeze student grants until inflation reduced them to loan levels and now proposes to cut them by 10 per cent every year for three years. Loans are to be increased proportionately. Yet loans can be seen as undermining the Robbins principle of state support for all students, though in the absence of a progressive tax system loans are also a way for higher earners to repay the educational investment that has supposedly been made in them. By 1996/7, the National Union of Students estimates loans will amount to £2,000 a year, leaving the average student on a three-year course owing £6,000 at graduation.

Flat-rate tuition fees have already been differentiated by subject area in an effort by government to go against the market they otherwise support and get higher education to take more science and technology students instead of the more popular arts and humanities enrolments. This makes some subjects more expensive to study than others, opening up the possibility for the introduction of top-up fees for prestigious courses and for some vocationally related ones.

The new system of funding, through the Councils for Further and Higher Education introduced by the 1992 Higher and Further Education Act, links central state support of universities and colleges to student numbers and this encouraged the dramatic rise in student intake; but this only explains the supply side of the equation. On the demand side, numbers enrolling for higher education have consistently outstripped targets set by government. And a demographic drop in the actual numbers of young people has increased the proportion of mature students. The source of this 'demand for HE remains a mystery', even according to Professor Peter Scott, former long-time editor of the sector's house journal, *The Times Higher Education Supplement*, in September 1992.

Yet, according to a large-scale survey undertaken for the

Department of Employment by Sheffield University in 1993, *Access, Entry and Potential Demand for Higher Education amongst 18–19 year olds in England and Wales*, 'There is still scope, amongst those who are "qualified" or "nearly qualified" for higher education, for more young people to be considered as part of the pool for recruitment to higher education'. Applications also continue to exceed admissions, especially after 1993 when the government suddenly got cold feet about its previous rapid expansion plans and withdrew funding for students in the more popular arts and humanities.

Despite the hardship this inflicted on students, who that year gained more 'A' level and other qualifying exam passes than ever before, the higher education institutions continued to cram the students in. Those who would previously have gained places at established universities were forced to go to former-polytechnics, while rejected applicants from these 'new universities' traded down again to the colleges of higher education. Admissions were also switched from already underfunded humanities and social sciences towards science and technology where new courses that could gain the full funding were started up. Other subjects – like psychology, for instance – redesignated themselves as sciences to attract additional full-funded students.

Education and the economy

The recent increase in student numbers still does not begin to approach the mass systems of higher education in other industrially developed countries, also invariably supported by loan systems. For example, the Netherlands, Sweden, the United States and Japan have over 80 per cent of their 18 year olds in education, a target at which the French are also aiming. This is not to mention newly industrialising countries like South Korea, which have already passed British levels. However, the sudden boost in student numbers seems a step along the way. It is a further, and perhaps inevitable, development from universal primary provision, through secondary schooling for all, towards the majority entering a tertiary level.

Moreover, expansion is justified by the generally accepted idea that as technology develops society demands more skilled and knowledgeable workers. More education and training for more people is therefore required to stay in the race with industrial competitors. Indeed, this idea had been accepted, at least in principle, ever since Britain's industrial primacy was first challenged in the last century by the French at the Paris exhibition of 1867 and then by the discoveries and development of the German chemical industry. It is a view exemplified by American President John F. Kennedy's remark, after the launch of the sputnik in 1957, that the US had to turn out greater numbers of Ph.D.s in order to surpass the Soviet Union in the space race.

Such long prevalent notions justifying an expansion of higher education are given additional currency by the equally widely accepted idea that a second industrial revolution is underway today. Spurred by the latest applications of computer electronics, society is supposedly progressing from a reliance upon the raw materials of nature to a new economy in which information is the sole source of wealth and power. History is thus alleged to have moved beyond industrialism, or at least beyond industry organised along the lines of mass production. This third phase of social evolution (following first agriculture and then industry) is accompanied by its own wave of technological development (microelectronics following petro-chemicals and the original iron and steel). So it is now seriously suggested by pundits that whole societies can exist by their members exchanging information with one another; and to do this everyone in a 'post-industrial' or 'information society' must acquire high level technical skills and theoretical knowledge. In this scenario it is not usually acknowledged that such societies can only exist at the expense of other, less advanced countries which have to supply them with food, fuel and manufactured goods.

Yet even if these speculations could be substantiated, it cannot be sufficiently emphasized that there is no empirically proven connection between economic performance and the levels of education in any given country. Education among the workforce of an enterprise is often irrelevant to on-the-job productivity and is sometimes counterproductive. This is indeed the case in Britain today where many graduates are forced to enter jobs for which they are 'overqualified'. They therefore feel dissatisfied, do a bad job and leave at the first better opportunity. So, while educational investment may sometimes be an enabling factor for productivity growth, the assertion that economic development necessarily follows from educational investment is a statement of pure faith. It is in fact more likely that in most cases educational improvements follow rather than lead to improved economic performance.

This is not to say that levels of technical competence among the workforce have no bearing on economic advance. In Germany, the country with which Britain is most often unfavourably compared in this respect, most workers are vocationally qualified – indeed, it is illegal to employ people for many jobs without such qualifications. In Britain, by contrast, most workers are still unqualified. General education standards are also lower. Graduate levels are similar however, both as regards quality and quantity, though less graduate in Britain in engineering and science. Differences lie in culture and work organisation – manual skill and technology in Germany are no less rewarded and no less a profession than what are generally regarded in Britain as 'better', non-manual careers. In fact, the German word for profession, *Beruf*, means also vocation or calling, as well as embracing the subtle discriminations the English make between occupation, trade, career and job.

More importantly though, there has also been the industrial investment in Germany that for long has been lacking in Britain to develop the skills of employees at work. For instance, it is estimated that 40 per cent of British graduates find employment at lower levels than those for which they are qualified. And the 1990 government report on 'Highly Qualified People' estimated that 'a degree was considered essential for only a third of the jobs to which employers had recently recruited new graduates'. The Department for Education's annual report showed that in England in 1992 only 49 per cent of students leaving colleges had found any kind of employment within the UK by the December following their graduation. *The Times Higher Education Supplement* reported in June 1993 that only 37 per cent of the previous year's graduates were in permanent employment after one year. Improving educational standards without people being able to apply what they know will not by itself improve the economy.

Certainly in the case of Britain's pioneering industrial revolution, the mass literacy and elementary schooling which industrial society is commonly supposed to require did not follow until a long time after the initial economic and technical advance. Not that we would argue for a return to the horrendous social conditions which obtained for the barely educated mass of the population in the nineteenth century; still less would we say that education is irrelevant to society. Indeed, we welcome the expansion of higher education, though not necessarily for the economic reasons commonly used to justify it – that it will enable us 'to catch up with our foreign competitors' and so inevitably 'raise living standards' for all. These do not necessarily follow.

Rather, we argue that the present partial moves towards a mass system of further and higher education for adults as well as younger people should be seen primarily as political responses to a new social situation. This involves the recomposition of the class structure that has been produced by the application of new technology in conditions of gowing economic insecurity. These moves towards mass further and higher education are encouraged by some government policies but not by others. What they do not represent is a rational response to current economic crisis and they cannot be justified by unfounded economic arguments. For to blame the failure of the economy upon a lack of education and training, as governments repeatedly have been doing since 1976, diverts attention from the real causes of Britain's declining position in competitive world markets, which is clearly due to underlying structural problems. This is clearly seen in relation to unemployment.

Permanent mass unemployment

Until recently employment went up and down with the recurrent booms and slumps of the trade cycle, as it has done ever since the inception of industrial capitalism. The rate of unemployment in Britain was never directly affected by productivity growth. This continued to lag behind that of other industrialised countries as the country rested upon the laurels of its initial competitive advantage and sheltered behind the protection of empire. These were the social and cultural factors that prevented any effective economic modernisation 'to catch up with our competitors'.

With the end of the long post-war boom in the 1973 oil crisis, the illusion was abandoned that unemployment had been permanently controlled by a Keynesian demand management of the economy. Permanent structural unemployment was accepted as part of the economic price to be paid for accommodation to a world economy in which British economic weakness was suddenly exposed. Rather than admit this openly, James Callaghan, the last Labour Prime Minister, in 1976 blamed the schools for the unemployment of school leavers.

Ever since, education and training have been presented as the cure-all for unemployment and the key to economic recovery and modernisation. The idea that investment in people (human capital) is more important than investment in plant and machinery (industrial capital) elevated the importance of education and training policies out of all proportion to their real place in the economy. This was especially true at a time when the economy was becoming increasingly globalised so that control over it was passing out of the hands of national governments, which came to depend upon investment by transnational corporations.

Despite the belief to which Callaghan's Ruskin speech gave currency, that specific skill shortages and a lack of general education were responsible for holding back economic advance, the permanent unemployment of millions is today tolerated as the price for controlling inflation. Skill shortages are not therefore the main constraint on economic growth. The major factor inhibiting increased output and employment is government reaction to inflationary tendencies in the economy as a whole, especially to wage demands. Until devaluation in October 1992 government response to any threat of a fall in the value of the pound was to jack up interest rates, choking off capital investment. Indeed, throughout the period of openly monetarist management of the economy since 1979 the critical level of unemployment which is regarded as 'the trigger' to 'fuel inflation' has been steadily raised. The threat of unemployment was thus used to damp down wage demands. Even when unemployment falls, general insecurity and widespread part-time working has the same effect. Meanwhile, the proportion of manufacturing firms reporting that the lack of skilled workers is holding back their industrial output is way below similar reports in the twenty years of virtually full employment in England after the war.

In the 1990s, upwards of four million people are denied the opportunity to develop any skills at work, or to apply their education and experience in employment. So the claim that a new 'post-industrial', 'information society' has been created, demanding higher skills and greater theoretical knowledge from all of its members sounds hollow to say the least. When the nature of the service sector employment that has replaced the two million-plus manufacturing jobs lost during the 1980s is examined, it also throws doubt on this claim.

The term services, as has been said, covers everything from

brain surgery to flipping hamburgers. Over half the growth in this area has been in managerial, administrative and financial services requiring higher qualifications, and the rest has been in occupations such as distribution, hotels and leisure, associated with low-paid, low-skilled employment. There has thus been a polarisation of employment, not the uniform upskilling of all work that is popularly presented as having occurred.

This reflects the wider economic and social 'restructuring' identified with the period of successive Thatcher governments, though the social changes they encouraged were the outcome of long-term trends that have yet to take final form. Basically, the traditional, tripartite social pyramid with distinct divisions between upper, middle and working classes has pulled apart. Paradoxically, this restructuring of class relationships may, for many people in the new middle of society, have reduced the awareness of material inequalities. Yet at the same time it has increased the distance between the two poles of richest and poorest.

All the social indicators show a widening of the gap between rich and poor since 1976, including the emergence of a more or less deliberately socially constructed and politically manipulated 'underclass' of the permanently unemployed. This resurrection of the 'rough' – as they were traditionally regarded by the 'respectable', skilled and regularly employed, working class – is a section of the old working class made dependent upon state benefits, policed by state agencies and relegated to the worst housing remaining to the local state – if housed at all. Living in relative poverty and at best employed part-time in insecure, semi-skilled jobs, the often racially and regionally stigmatised 'underclass' forms a pool of labour to be drawn upon as flexible demands dictate. Educationally the 'underclass' is marked by lack of formal qualifications and by unwilling participation in successive vocational training and make-work schemes, more recently involving work-for-benefit.

The education of the new middle-working class

Meanwhile in the middle of society, the previously clear cut distinction between the non-manual middle class and the manual working class has been eroded by the growth of services, especially in offices and selling. The latest applications of new technology have also replaced many of the hard labouring jobs of the past.

This has led to a confused situation in which many people see themselves not as part of the traditional working or middle classes but as individuals in a new middle, or working-middle of society. Different from the ruling class 'Them' or 'The rich' above, but also dutifully employed, Conservative voting and desperately mortgage paying, they are increasingly willing, if not always able, to take out private medical insurance and to pay for private schooling to safeguard themselves and their children from falling into the social abyss of the educationally uncertificated, state-dependent and growing 'underclass' beneath them. Society thus moves towards the widely predicted two-thirds : one-third pattern of securely employed core against a poor and insecurely employed, peripheral 'underclass'.

Yet during the same period when these new social patterns became apparent, insecurity has been heightened for all employees and the self-employed (the latter growing from 442,000 in 1971 to 3,222,000 by 1990), as well as for many small employers and business managers. Not only has everyone been affected by the increasingly marginal status of the British economy in crisis-ridden world markets, but also new methods of management and administration have been introduced at the same time. This 'enterprise culture' has permeated all levels of society except the real core of the employing class, who hold interlinked directorships and dominant share-holdings in the largest financial, commercial and (what remain of) industrial enterprises, and who are still drawn, with few exceptions, from a very narrow elite, upper or ruling class. Growing insecurity for the rest heightens the importance of qualifications as supposed guarantees of permanent, core employment, increasing the demand for education that many in the new working-middle of society are willing to pay – or at least become indebted – for.

The 'enterprise solution' to Britain's problems was advanced by Mrs Thatcher's governments as a new form of modernisation and a way out of the apparent dead-end of corporate capitalism. The old mixed economy, between private and state capital, was replaced by a new mixed economy, of state-subsidised private capital and semi-privatised state capital. The operational principal of this new enterprise state is one of franchise, in which, like a holding company, parts are subcontracted out to be run independently by franchise holders on fixed, short-term, target-specific contracts. Civil service bureaucracies can thus be expanded and disbanded to meet demand. This leaves, as in the private sector, a securely employed core surrounded by a growing periphery of workers on short-term contracts. The new type of state is thus 'contracting' in two senses – at the centre where power is concentrated and in its 'contracting' mode of operation by franchising to independent agencies. In the often heavily state-subsidised private sector too, processes of managerial decentralisation and labour-shedding have broken up former corporate monoliths into their semi-autonomous constituent units acting independently to adapt flexibly to rapidly changing market conditions.

'Enterprise', operating through the franchise or contract principle, has also been applied, as will be seen, to the management of education at all levels. But it is the new social situation, briefly outlined above, that has given education a heightened significance for many people in the new working-middle of society. This new situation can be compared with education in traditional, tripartite society as it was re-established after the second world war. Then the schools and colleges were rigidly stratified. The upper class were educated privately and intensively from an early age through a succession of nurses, nannies, preparatory and boarding schools to an extended childhood at sheltered Oxbridge colleges, finishing schools and military academies from which they moved effortlessly on to leadership in society and the state. Beneath them, the grammar schools and Civic universities were seen as vocationally serving the middle class, which had grown over the course of the nineteenth century, by preparing them for non-manual, professional occupations. Working-class children, also following a pattern consolidated in Victorian times, left school as early as possible and boys sought to gain apprenticeships in secure, skilled, manual trades. Apprenticeships came to be supplemented by night-schools, technical colleges and eventually – after 1964 – by polytechnics.

Although there was some movement post-1945, it did not disrupt the prewar pattern. In the traditional universities this ordered educational world was reflected in the division between 'first class minds', upper and lower second and third class degree classification. For at all levels of education only a minority progressed to the next stage. Failure for the majority was the norm, teaching them their place in the hierarchy.

Since 1979 many of the successive Conservative governments' education reforms aimed to reintroduce grammar schooling and harked back to this ideal selection of an elite. However, the logic

of the contracting out of school education through local management of funds supplied by the centre is towards a state-subsidised
privatisation that could eventually put all schools on the same
financial footing as the private schools, though without their
inherited privileged position at the top of the market. The parallel
effects of the market in higher education are explored in the
contrasted educational experiences that are the subject of this
book.

The market reform of education

The process of marketing schools to compete as individual agencies for students funded from the centre pioneered and paralleled
what has been called the market modernisation of the new enterprise state. This followed the precedent set by the Manpower
Services Commission for the Department of Employment's previous funding of Youth Training. During the 1980s, the MSC paid
the agencies managing YTS on a *per capita* basis for each trainee
they attracted to their schemes. In such a system of semi-private
agencies, each training organisation, school or college receives
central government grants according to the number of trainees/
pupils/students it gains in competition with its rivals. The independent schools could have no objections eventually to joining
such a state system in which they would still be able to select
pupils and charge fees. In return, they would receive government
grants for every pupil they already had. Instead of the state taking
over the private sector, as Labour had always advocated if not
implemented, Mrs Thatcher's intention was to subsidise the privatisation of the public sector. The division between private and
public would then be lost in the competition between state-
subsidised independent institutions. This was indeed Mrs
Thatcher's vision of what one of her education ministers called a
'new partnership between parents and the state'.

The eventual outcome of this independent budgeting would be
to strengthen the position of already 'successful' schools and colleges, while the market forces of parental choice would close the
'least successful'. At the same time schools could begin to charge
fees for more facilities or 'extras' – as the 1987 Education Act put
it. As in the private schools sector, 'extras' might soon include
better equipment, smaller classes and more qualified teachers
attracted by higher salaries; while in the colleges only the better-

off students would be able to afford the more expensive courses at prestigious departments in the most renowned institutions (predictably at the antique universities).

The testing of children at seven, eleven, fourteen and sixteen was intended to provide an indication to parents of the 'success' or otherwise of competing schools. For that reason test results had to be simplified down to raw scores in a few basic spelling and maths exercises. The importance of such arbitrary educational selection is heightened by the growing insecurity about employment prospects that has been noted, even for the top 20 per cent of school leavers who were previously guaranteed access to careers in supervisory/administrative, non-manual employment by good school performance. Now that degree level higher education is required for entry to more and more professional/managerial occupations – indeed increasingly, to secure employment of any sort – there is greater dependence upon academic achievement as the means of reproducing superior status, with greater resort by those who can afford it to private schooling.

Further, educational credentials assume a new importance in achieving or sustaining cultural distinctions in the absence of clear-cut divisions between the formerly manual working class and the traditionally non-manual middle class. This is the origin of today's accelerating 'credential inflation' or 'diploma devaluation', as it has been called. Long ago, the French educational sociologist Pierre Bourdieu pointed out how culturally arbitrary qualifications can change their worth as badges of distinction acquired by different social groups, and how new signs of exclusion can be elaborated by traditional elites to preserve privileged access to the powerful positions they previously inherited but which are now ostensibly open to meritocratic competition.

Especially for those who think of themselves, and would like to think of their children, as traditionally 'middle' rather than 'working' class, educational credentials have a new significance. The lack of any certification is a virtual condemnation to the dependency of the 'underclass' and exclusion from the new, respectable working-middle of society. Parental demand thus contributes to the widening differentiation between state schools that the Education Reform Act was designed to encourage.

Meanwhile in this academic competition, the attempt to construct a vocationally relevant education for the rest of the school population has been abandoned. Britain's long period of dithering between following the German 'dual' system of minority grammar schooling with the majority in apprenticeships, and an American model of general school education to 18 with access for as many as possible to higher education thereafter, seems to have been resolved in favour of a very academic, narrow and traditional version of the latter. The policy changed abruptly after the 1987 election and the subsequent 1988 Education Act. The proportions were reversed and the majority of young people, previously expected to join vocational Youth Training, were now supposed to stay on for academic study at school or college with only a minority dropping out to Youth Training, which was redefined as a sort of expanded special education.

In these new circumstances, the framework of National Vocational Qualifications (NVQs), designed to accredit both academic and vocational qualifications in one unitary system, has little to do with building the 'ladders and bridges' for progression and access for all, or with creating the skills needed for economic modernisation. Rather, the NVQs help to extend still further the period during which young people and others are removed from the labour market, to be certified on courses of non-training and non-education for non-jobs. This outcome of expanding further and higher education in a recession became clearer as the Dearing Review of the 'national' curriculum was published in 1994. This rejected the attempt to impose a grammar school curriculum upon all school pupils in favour of a resuscitated tripartite system with three streams at 16-plus, of NVQs, General NVQs and 'A' levels. For those at school and FE in these last two top streams, still further discrimination and disqualification is emerging in the new hierarchy of higher education.

Higher education in a new state

The new hierarchy of colleges and universities

Previously, beyond the cuts of the early 1980s, the minority and elitist English higher education system had been relatively unaffected by the changes inflicted upon the rest of education by successive Conservative regimes. An academic minority continued to be selected for education to a high level. Selection was only apparently meritocratic for it favoured those from the traditional upper and non-manual middle classes. Standards however were high and drop-out was low.

At the end of the 1980s the Tories eventually got around to addressing the sector with a series of measures, beginning with the introduction of student loans. The new situation in higher education created by the 1992 Further and Higher Education Act can be seen as providing a model for the type of differentiated market that the government hopes to replicate in schools as well as further education. Indeed, only minor changes were necessary to produce such a competitive hierarchy, as an elaborate pecking-order of universities already existed. There was also already a submerged market in higher education, in which independent, self-governing universities competed with their various specialised course offerings for state-subsidised students. The removal of the binary division between universities and polytechnics, though welcome in the name of equality, completed this differentiated hierarchy; and at the same time it removed the last vestiges of local accountability and democratic control over higher education.

Despite funding from the centre for individual departments and cost centres within them, which tends to break up institutions, it is predictable that, with the introduction (also in the 1992 Act) of separate costing for research and teaching, which will lead to the concentration of research in specialist centres, there will be a new binary divide as the universities at the bottom of the pile become teaching-only institutions. Here 'skills' courses narrowly related to employment will be concentrated, along with two-year degree programmes. The former are encouraged by the Department of Employment's higher education version of its earlier Technical and Vocational Education Initiative for schools. The latter are at present being piloted in 11 former-polytechnics – for adult (25-plus) students only so far.

At the other pole of the widening spectrum are courses unrelated to any specific employment but serving as a cultural apprenticeship to higher management positions in business and finance, to top positions in the media and the core of civil service administration. Such courses also pander to the academic consumerism of some overseas students and those who can afford to study for intrinsic interest alone. In place of flat-rate fees that are the same for all courses, fees raised to the full cost of such prestigious courses can be anticipated as colleges in the antique universities and elsewhere may be tempted to privatise themselves out of the state system. As they have done before, they may also raise their entry requirements to preserve their elite status rather than admit more students who meet their old standards. Increased business sponsorship of individual students through courses at all levels can also be expected.

The quality of course validation is therefore vital to preserving even any pretence of equality and commonality of academic culture in the new HE. In the past a monitoring body called the Council for National Academic Awards (CNAA) ensured that the degrees of all the non-incorporated colleges and polytechnics were comparable with university degrees. These were independently assessed by the various university corporations, supplemented by systems of external examination for each others' academic awards. All graduate and postgraduate degrees were therefore officially supposed to be equivalent to each other. Within the system this may have been the case, more or less.

Most employers though, save for the few degrees that specifically match their special technical requirements, have always looked more favourably on Oxbridge degrees, especially for management posts, and rank HE institutions thereafter. So no matter how vocationally relevant the course that applicants had followed at polytechnic they are unlikely to be considered for many high status jobs. Thus, although within academia all degrees were officially held to be equal, outside of it some degrees were demonstrably more equal than others. Nevertheless, there did previously exist a formal equality between degrees; even this seems now set to disappear.

With the abolition of the CNAA in 1993, all the universities in the new system can award their own degrees and already there are accusations that standards are slipping. It may therefore be necessary to reinvent a CNAA for all degree-awarding HEIs. This may accompany the introduction of 'core curricula' for basic, two-year degree programmes in many subjects. Indeed, the NVQ core skills of numeracy, literacy, familiarity with information technology and so-called 'personal and transferable skills' already constitute such a common core for all subjects to levels 4 and 5 (equals degree and Masters level). Ironically however, the most prestigious universities will assert their distinctive claims to 'quality' by opting out of such 'national' curricula and continuing with traditional three-year degrees, just as the universities in the past made much of their Royal Charters of independence from regulation by the former CNAA. The move to twice-yearly semesters or year-round trimesters in place of three archaically named terms facilitates two-year modular degrees. Resistance to this change may provide the standard which universities seeking to assert that they are not merely teaching-only institutions may raise, to signal their adherence to a traditional elite. Indeed, there was some evidence for this in our interviews with staff at what we have called Home Counties University (see chapter three).

Common standards are however all the more necessary as, with more courses broken down into modular components that carry credits equivalent to each other, students can more easily transfer from course to course and from institution to institution. Semesters of the same length at all colleges will also facilitate this transfer. Despite the loyalty that students usually show to their college, individual students may be tempted to 'trade up' the system, from less to more prestigious courses and colleges. Elite institutions will then safeguard themselves by raising entry qualifications and retaining their own term system out of sync with the majority. As in the USA, only an Ivy League of the top colleges will then be regarded as 'real education', even though what they teach may well be increasingly academic and remote from reality. Mass universities for the many will then be combined with elite universities for the few.

In this worst of both worlds, with the resulting competition all down the line to shadow the medieval flummery and academic obscurantism of Oxford and Cambridge, the distinctive contributions of the former-polytechnics could be lost, just as the ideals of the comprehensive schools are being submerged in the academic competition engendered by the 1988 Act. Meanwhile, in the forgotten college sector of HE, colleges that do not attain university status will merge or close. This may also be the fate of those new universities that lose out in the competition for students and research funds. Mergers in their cases may be accompanied by collapse into regional learning centres ranged around the surviving management core of the old institutions.

Further Education colleges in competition with sixth form colleges and schools may also tend towards merger as their funding arrangements favour large institutions. Others could be absorbed in the universities from which they franchise the initial level of degree courses, and to which they feed students. It is indeed impossible to speak any longer of further, or even adult, education separately from higher education: a *de facto* further and higher education system now exists for adults as well as for younger people post-16, even though the 1992 Further and Higher Education Act formally separated them in two nominally distinct sectors for the first time.

Opportunities and challenges

Neither the form that the extension of this new system of further and higher education will take nor its curricular content is fixed; it should also be recalled that the previous and more modest expansion of HE coincided with the student unrest of the late 1960s (and that of FE and Youth Training with the urban riots of the early 1980s). Although the 1960s student rebellions were associated with a very different period, of expansion and relative prosperity, they were, as much as anything else, a product of the frustrated expectations of a generation of students, the majority of whose parents had not attended HE, and for whom promises of access to new and more demanding job opportunities were unlikely to be met. With continued stagnation of the economy, the same frustration is likely to recur, only this time, if targets are reached, for the far larger numbers graduating indebted and unemployed. Thus, education without jobs in the 1990s is in the process of replacing the training without jobs of the 1970s and 1980s.

Despite the chronic practical difficulties the rapid multiplication of student numbers poses for overstretched institutions, the expansion of higher education presents HE staff with opportunities to assist greater numbers of students to gain access to a culture of critical, scientific reason and generalised – as opposed to vocational – knowledge.

Patterns of education and qualification are changing fundamentally, because more pupils from all backgrounds are staying on at school. Many take 'A' levels in sixth form, rather than NVQs or BTEC in FE and, even though nearly a third of them fail or drop out from 'A' levels, since grades are norm referenced, more entrants means more passes with more eligible for university or college entrance (even though government and some colleges arbitrarily vary the entry requirements by subject year on year). Added to these rising numbers of 'A' level entrants are students accepted through access courses, or with the GNVQs or BTEC qualifications that many higher education institutions accept, at least in principle, as 'A' level equivalents. So, if one third of the age range, as well as many more adults, can be helped to think creatively, logically and independently by their higher education experiences, this represents a major cultural change for society.

This also presents a challenge to the traditional academic culture of higher education itself. More, as everybody keeps saying, means different. For the courses offered to these larger numbers and new types of student cannot be the same as the three- or four-year finishing school experience previously enjoyed by an academic, traditionally middle-class elite who were culturally prepared for it by their preceding schooling.

The previous and limited expansion of HE following Robbins, although it accommodated more working-class students in absolute numbers, hardly shifted the proportions from manual and non-manual families. These divisions have been sustained, as the recent demographic fall in numbers of young people has not affected the traditional middle class as much as it has manual workers. At the end of the 1980s over two-thirds of the take-up of full-time higher education was still from social classes 1 and 2, while only one per cent of full-time HE students were the children of unskilled workers.

But with the decline of manual occupations and the expansion of non-manual ones there is now a change in the overall class composition of students. Higher education of some sort has already become available beyond the exceptional 'scholarship boy' to the children of parents who would not themselves have considered remaining in education after school. For these new entrants, negative 'push' factors (no jobs) are complemented by positive 'pull' factors as a higher education experience becomes more widely prized for its biographical significance as well as for its value in the labour market.

For women too, the female majority staying on at school and in FE is working its way through to higher education. The new technology which has reduced the need for manual labour is reducing the differences between what was formerly 'men's and women's work'. More and more women work in full-time careers for longer periods of their lives in relationships where both partners have to find employment to maintain an adequate standard of living. There is thus a forceful lobby for equal opportunities, challenging the tendency for certain courses, like languages and sociology for example, to become feminized and thus academically devalued. More women are also entering former male preserves such as the 'hard' sciences, maths and economics.

Given the 4.8 per cent average ethnic minority population of the UK (though higher for the younger generation), black and Asian participation in HE is already high at 10.45 per cent of all admissions in 1990. However, this conceals differences in attendance for different institutions – the former-polytechnic and college sector admitting more black and Asian people than the old universities. As with women, the more prestigious the institution and the course, the fewer ethnic minorities attend. There is also great variation in the proportions of students from different ethnic groups applying to different types of course. Further, partly because many black students are mature entrants with families to support, preliminary investigation suggests drop-out from courses is likely to be higher for them.

To class, gender and race could be added disability. An estimated 0.3 per cent of higher education students are recorded as disabled, although they are 3 per cent of the 21–29 age group. These combinations of disadvantage produce a familiar pattern in which the more elite courses and institutions preserve their predominantly middle-class, male and white composition behind a liberal rhetoric of equal opportunities. This impeccable facade makes it difficult to even discuss with them the possibility of unequal treatment, let alone begin to do something about it – by implementing basic monitoring for example.

These are all challenges for the new higher education. There are also new opportunities for new courses using the latest information technology to communicate concepts and information in new ways. Traditional subject boundaries are crumbling as the databases of previously discrete disciplines are interrelated by the new technology as well as by the latest scientific discoveries. Professors and lecturers fearful of losing their formerly specialised knowledge or expertise are recast as the 'facilitators' of their students' independent learning. They face losing their students' former dependence upon them and see themselves relegated to the role of technicians or auxiliaries (see chapter three).

All these changes in higher education and the social situation which has produced them have upset traditional English preferences. These privilege 'higher' over 'lower' order skills, intellectual abstraction over mechanical application, formal rationality and articulacy over the tacit and inarticulate knowledge on which reasoning consciousness is founded. Such prejudices merely preserve a conventional social preference for mental over manual labour. This dates back to the Ancient Greek scorn for slave labour, reinforced by the medieval Christian ideal of abstract contemplation and polished up by the Victorian cult of gentlemanly amateurism. These ingredients were vital to the development of universities and their cherished independence of inquiry and critical thought. They too will have to be rethought and find new expression in the new universities and colleges of the future.

The proletarianisation of the professions

Academic professors

The much-cherished independence of the universities has been central to their ideal image of themselves as developed in Europe since the Renaissance. Their autonomous self-government supposedly safeguarded the freedom of inquiry of members of the academic community. However, in Britain since the second world war their increasing reliance upon state funding undermined these pretensions to independence. University Vice Chancellors therefore had little option but to succumb to the Conservative government's demand at the end of the 1980s that a market-driven expansion of higher education should take place in the 1990s.

Such compliance was nothing new. Despite the cultivated eccentricities of the odd professor or two and the individual conditions of much academic work, academic life at universities is in general marked by the respectable conventionality and social conformity of its staff. For in the academic world individuals' professional positions are based upon their reputation amongst the 'invisible college' of their peers. This 'peer review' system, despite its ethos of dedication to pure research and scholarship, in practice often stifles originality, preserves outdated subject subdivisions and only serves to encourage academic careerism fostered by professorial paternalism (again, see chapter three).

Reputation amongst their peers, which individual academics pursue supposedly for its own sake, is after all linked to financial reward, not only in terms of salaries, which are low relative to other professional occupations, but also to sometimes lucrative private consultancies. There are also the perks of a previously secure and comfortable existence – if not company cars, then trips abroad to conferences, sabbaticals and exchange visits, etc. Meanwhile, much of the day to day work of teaching and research in universities is sustained by postgraduate students and a growing army of insecurely employed contract staff who now make up to a third of all academic employees.

The threat to their previously relatively privileged way of life has prompted dons' recent hostility to Conservative government. Its policies are seen as undermining the professional ideal not only of academics themselves but also of the professions for which they prepare their students. Central to this conception of a profession is the expert and specialised knowledge which higher education imparts.

Self-regulation by its own members is a stronger definition for a profession than the mere possession of specialist knowledge – a criterion for exclusivity also shared by skilled craftworkers. As policed by the British Medical Association, the Royal College of Nurses or the Law Society, doctors, nurses and lawyers exert greater control over their situation than either teachers or journalists, for example. In the older universities, and the newer ones modelled on them, anarchic and archaic forms of collegial self-government by the academic community of fellows also still perform this function for academics. In the Civic universities erected from Victorian times on a German model of subject specialisation, and in the former technical universities, departmental rule by the professorate is bolstered by 'peer review' systems of maintaining professional integrity. The two forms of management – collegial and departmental – are both opposed to the top-down corporate management structures imposed upon staff in the former-polytechnics, who see themselves as being reduced to teaching functionaries. In the new competitive market, this model is being borrowed from the former-polytechnics to spread to other higher education institutions.

In whichever section or former-section of higher education, intrusion by the state is resented. One national survey showed support for the Conservative Party amongst academics dropping from 48 per cent in 1963 to under 20 per cent in 1992 (15 per cent at Oxbridge). The same study also found that most academics would prefer a post at Oxbridge to a higher paying position in another university. This shows how the Oxbridge ideal still dominates the self-conception of academics.

From its crown of academic reputation, Oxbridge sends out

graduates to top positions at the other universities so that they tend to conform to its original image. This process explains much of the 'academic drift' in institutions like the Victorian Civic universities, or the later technical universities. They have both veered away from their original mission of serving local industry, towards a predominant emphasis upon the liberal arts. This process was paralleled by a concentration of the age range on young men and women living on campus in term time as a transitional stage in moving from home. For instance, two thirds of Sheffield University students were in 1907 local, part-time and mainly adult evening students, a proportion which was subsequently more than reversed.

By contrast, the new universities of the 1960s were deliberately built on the outskirts of cathedral towns for their new 18–21 year old expanding middle-class clientele, as arts institutions cloned from their Oxbridge originals. There is already evidence that the former-polytechnics converted to universities are tending in the same direction, not only by adopting the pseudo-rituals of academic gowns and titles but by advertising their new student residences as equivalent to the residential college and campus experiences they distantly shadow.

The professional class

Oxbridge not only endorses the academic profession but also forms an essential part of the status symbolism of all English elites. The ancient colleges were originally founded to train the medieval professions of the clergy, medicine and law. In the nineteenth century, with the availability of cheap, mass-produced paper, the examinations for the First Division of the Civil Service were closely modelled on the Oxbridge honours papers, even though at that time the majority of Oxbridge students habitually left without bothering to take any examinations at all. They had derived sufficient gentlemanly experience just by being there for a period. As a result, a bachelor's (sic) degree was little more than a certificate of residence and good behaviour for three years and collecting it was only important for those who wanted to become bishops or masters of a college. (These latter had already failed in any case by being the second or third, instead of the first and inheriting son in their family. On the distinction between rulers, such as the old feudal aristocrats, and those who rule, mandarin-like, on behalf of the Emperor, see Marx's division between 'the ruling class' and 'the governing caste'.)

Yet by 1900, as the exam system spread, it had become virtually impossible for non-Oxbridge graduates to reach senior positions in church or state, in law or in the private schools feeding pupils to individual Oxbridge colleges. Harold Perkin's history of 'The Rise of Professional Society' thus describes the two antique universities as 'the main articulator of the social ideal of the professional class'.

In industry and commerce the rise of 'the professional class' was also linked to the growth of paperwork. The application of Taylorism to automate and deskill industrial processes translated the knowledge of craftworkers from the shopfloor onto flowcharts and schedules on paper in the office. Here middle managers did not, unlike the original managers of private companies, own the enterprise but could claim authority based instead upon specialised knowledge. This came to be validated by higher education qualifications but it was not until after the second world war that it was common for English engineers and business managers to possess formal graduate-level qualifications.

With the growth of higher education, degrees have become necessary for the parallel growth of a range of occupations which have closed themselves off from non-graduate applicants. Degrees were also increasingly required for administrators and other professionals in the growing organisations of the welfare state founded after the war. So, alongside 'the working class', a whole 'thinking class', dealing in more or less abstract knowledge grew up, especially in the media and advertising but also in teaching and research. The training for employment of this 'thinking class' includes the higher education that develops their high levels of literacy together with their general reasoning abilities.

The growth of graduate-entry careers, which still continues, has been aided by the latest applications of new technology. This has prompted new demands less for the specific vocational skills acquired within particular companies and other organisations and more for general abilities and knowledge taught in schools and colleges. These so-called 'personal, transferable skills' are actually generic or universal competences required in a variety of work situations rendered increasingly identical by the similar use of information technology and by similar forms of work reorganisation.

Because information technology is now being applied in employment and education at a later stage than its initial development in industry, it is no longer being used primarily to automate and deskill work processes and learning. Rather, its use at all levels of training and education is part of a process of making formerly specialised information more generally available to new members of the workforce as well as retraining old ones. This information-generating (and generalising) capacity of information technology has the effect of opening up the formerly specialised knowledge of office managers and reintegrating their functions with routine work. This places new skill demands upon what remains of the core workforce in employment at the same time as it undermines the position of professional middle managers.

In higher education similar processes are at work, encouraged by the new forms of work organisation that involve all academics in the administration and accounting of their own professional labour. Access to privileged knowledge is an aspect of professionalism likely to have been stressed by higher education teachers when defining their teaching in compliance with the requirements of professional bodies; and increasingly, when defining their own work according to externally specified measures of 'quality'. In addition, previously discrete subject disciplines are being inter-related by the latest scientific discoveries as well as by new technology. As formerly specialised databases become accessible to information about other aspects of reality, academic experts, who had previously carved out a specialised niche for themselves in the intricate division of knowledge that used to obtain, find themselves suddenly exposed.

The academic specialisms that are now breaking down were originally a by-product of the increasing availability of free time in a society that was becoming more and more productive. The Victorian gentleman amateur, who pursued his own research interest irrespective of where it led, eventually gave way to the professional scientist and scholar. Industry and the state needed to organise research and inquiry but usually could not do so directly since research is by its nature unpredictable. As Mrs Thatcher – herself for a short time employed as a research chemist – told the Parliamentary and Scientific Committee in 1989: 'The greatest economic benefits of scientific research have always resulted from advances in fundamental knowledge rather than the search for specific applications.'

On the other hand, the public funding of research, as well as education at all levels and indeed health and other social services, means that those who work in these areas have some public accountability for what they do and cannot be left just to follow their own bent. They can however, if they can make their voices heard, justify their actions in a way that is not open to employees of private companies who are directly accountable only to their employer. Private sector workers are therefore much more immediately constrained by short-term demands for their product in the commercial market-place.

This was an additional reason for privatising public work as far as Conservative governments were concerned. For Mrs Thatcher and her successors rejected the old consensual management of the former mixed economy in favour of a new mix in which a state-subsidised private sector dominates a semi-privatised state sector. If, as part of their accompanying market modernisation of the economy, market mechanisms could be got to determine demand for public sector products and services, this would remove them from the arena of public debate and democratic determination. There would then be no further discussion of their purposes, which would become, like everything else, merely to maximise the return they could earn in the market.

The market in ideas

The dedication that successive Conservative governments showed to the principals of early-nineteenth century, neo-liberal economics, in which social problems and priorities were supposed to be resolved by the hidden hand of market forces, is difficult to apply to the field of ideas, particularly the generation of new ideas. Universities are very observant of intellectual ownership rights so that most discoveries belong to the university not to the individual. Many of them employ a full-time specialist to deal with this issue and often little else. Nevertheless, it is notoriously tricky to patent the ownership of an idea and the applications of new knowledge are not easily harnessed merely to the production of commodities for sale. Moreover, new discoveries and new connections with old ones cannot be unmade and today they are ever more easily stored, retrieved, communicated and expressed in a variety of media.

The dynamic of the world of ideas is thus irrepressible. New knowledge reveals new possibilities and is, as has been said, always liable to overstep the bounds of the society that created and now seeks to contain it, in order to preserve the conditions of its own social existence. Original acts of creation and discovery – and learning about or rediscovering them – are not only enjoyable because they engage people's natural curiosity and imagination, but are also always implicitly critical of the world as it is because they have created something new and potentially upsetting for the existing state of affairs. This poses acute problems for those who wish to maintain things as they are and to use the latest scientific discoveries, artistic and literary creations and theoretical ideas in order to do so.

There are different options available to a capitalist society to resolve this difficult relationship. The need to resolve it is the more pressing as industry becomes ever more science based. Scientific research is not only becoming more expensive but is increasingly integrated with production. Private corporations can therefore set up their own research institutes, either singly or collectively, as in the USA where companies also sponsor charitable foundations dedicated to medical and other research. Or the state can subsidise research centres to support the needs of national industry, as in Japan.

Another possibility is for companies to apply the rhetoric of themselves becoming educational institutions, constantly learning to develop new products and teaching their employees in order to do so. In-house training would then develop beyond awarding its own certification of mechanical competence, to giving the company's own degrees for higher level technical and also management staff. British Telecom has already been granted the authority to do this by the former-CNAA, while British Leyland at Coventry is moving in the same direction. BL is supported by local universities even though they may thus end up doing themselves out of business, at least as far as some of their engineering students are concerned.

In the past, when two universities supplied virtually all the scientists and intellectuals who were required in England and Wales, these ancient institutions could be allowed to get along with little supervision by the state. Even as the universities grew in number they were given room to pursue relatively pure research in the different areas in which they specialised. But with much more money being required from the public purse for increasingly expensive research projects, there was a growing demand for accountability over how it was being spent, especially as there was also greater competition for dwindling public funds. This is another reason for the pressure upon higher education to conform to the demands of the market modernisation of the economy, as well as for academics to become part of it themselves by self-financing, selling their services at a profit in the market.

In the area of arms production there has always been a close and mutually beneficial link between universities, the military and the arms industry. The Ministry of Defence particularly has long been a good tap for research funds, especially as their mismanagement is legendary – so much so that geographers have attributed a large part of the growth of defence-related precision electronics in the formerly prosperous South East of England to adjacent university research departments. With the end of the cold war some winding down in this area can be anticipated, though much of Britain's 'export success' continues to depend upon arms sales (estimated at 20 per cent of the country's export earnings).

In a world economy dominated by trans-national corporations based in the most powerful countries – the USA, Japan and the heartland of Europe – industrial research no less than production is internationalised. So the universities in the industrially developed countries are shifting from guardians of national knowledge to ancillaries in the production of knowledge for global corporations. This, as well as their financial dependence upon the state, is making it difficult for many of them to sustain their previous commitment to independent research, vital though it is to the self-concept of the professionals who work in them and to their traditional ideal of a university.

The academic community – if it is possible to speak of such a thing – thus feels beleaguered not only by the state, but also by the market and the economy, all of which exert a more and more direct influence over higher education in place of the indirect effects they had previously. The assimilation of the universities by these external forces is partial and incomplete, taking various forms across different institutions and the various subjects and modes of study within them. The polarities of the process are illustrated however, in our comparison of two contrasted universities today, between full-time studentship in traditional subjects on a residential campus compared with part-time programmes in the locality built around work-based learning.

In the traditional ideal of a university – derived ultimately from the Ancient Greeks – students are supposed to benefit from a withdrawal from the world to be taught by experts at the leading edge of scientific discovery, scholarly research and theoretical elaboration. The wisdom of the sage is presumed, in some undefined way, to transmit itself to the initiates gathered around him, just as it did to Sophocles' acolytes all those years ago. Seminars and tutorials too are traditionally modelled upon the Socratic dialogues of question and answer in Plato's symposium.

But students universally complain that their teachers are less interested in teaching them than in the research upon which their academic reputation depends. Indeed, pedagogy (the science – or is it an art? – of teaching and learning) has been neglected in the old universities. This is because there is little career potential in being recognised as a good teacher, and because in the way that learning is organised in the old universities and those modelled on them, responsibility for failure rests with the individual student not the poor standards of their teachers. As a result, in their senior common rooms teaching is often a dirty word and the government's present preference for the separation of teaching from research is being strenuously resisted.

Enterprising attitudes

The government's intentions have been clearly signalled in the redesignation of the Department of Education and Science as the Department for Education, science being hived off to a special cabinet office. Further savings will be made in the state funding of research – especially major and costly scientific projects – with their concentration in a few specialist centres, with perhaps as few as ten universities in a research-university superleague separate from the mass of teaching-only institutions. This pruning will further erode the relatively weak research base of the country and predictably encourage the 'brain drain' that has accelerated over recent years. In any case, many of the best scientists already work in industry so that it is often difficult to recruit them to lower salaries in universities.

Some of the corporate managers of the new universities (formerly polytechnics) are as fiercely opposed as their long-time university counterparts to the separation of teaching from research. They are as reluctant as the non-Ivy League universities to becoming confirmed as teaching-only institutions and are demanding that they be given equal shares with the established universities in the present levels of research funding. However, they are in general less conservative – with a small c – than their colleagues in the older universities. They have already gained from the new dispensation and are confident that they can win more in free market competition.

For them the new situation affords the opportunity to create a new learning society in which professional knowledge would be generalised to everybody. For the first time formal, academic study could be related to practical, applied learning in a unified vocational system. This would aim at demolishing the traditional divisions between selection for an elite education for the professions and practical training for technicians and the crafts. At the same time more open and meritocratic social relations could promote the modernisation and revitalisation of the economy.

There is a further discussion of this idea in chapter five but for now suffice it to say that unfortunately, because this vision of a learning society is typically posed in purely technical terms, it ignores the historical realities of culture and class. As expressed by corporate managers in the US business school language of 'functional role analysis', it too often lets slip the bottom line of their 'mission statements', which is always to maximize profits.

Even here though, especially at the level at which organisational change begins to impinge upon traditional divisions of status and authority within companies and higher education institutions as corporations, established authorities are unwilling to substantiate the rhetoric of their employment demands. Employers typically ask for employees, graduates especially, who have 'initiative', 'responsibility', 'the ability to learn to learn' and suchlike. They also demand that all employees be 'flexible' and 'adaptive', and even that they not expect 'a job for life' – at least not with the same company.

These interchangeable terms can mean different things at different levels of employment. For some, they present the opportunity to develop their portfolios of achievements and experiences, acquiring further 'personal and transferable skills' before moving on to more lucrative contracts and consultancies on an independent, self-contracting basis. For others, they mean putting up with insecure employment, without pension and other regular employment benefits and protection, temporary contracts, low wages, mind-numbing boredom, disgusting conditions and degrading treatment.

Although the most effective use of new technology blurs the fundamental division between manual and mental work, shop-floor and office, operator and manager, the personal investment in managerial authority is just too great for corporations even to begin becoming learning organisations much beyond the level of middle management. It is not only material interests in career positions in the hierarchy that are at stake but also ideological conviction in the whole purpose of working to produce a profit regardless of other social considerations. This would be thrown into question by a genuine participation of the majority of the workforce in learning to manage all the enterprises in the economy.

The aspiration for professional education for all in a learning society therefore remains largely rhetorical. It would imply not only higher education for all but careers for all. The social implications of taking such a slogan seriously challenge deeply-engrained hierarchies of interest and habit. They are too far-reaching for the powers that be to entertain seriously.

Students thus face conflicting demands between appeals to quality that reproduce the traditional academic definitions of excellence in highly specialised courses and the claims to general vocational relevance of mixed and wider degree courses. They are faced with penetrating the real relevance of often obscure traditional studies as well as the rhetoric of relevance to a range of employments offered by new courses and methods of study.

'Flexibility' and 'adaptability' are the keywords of the new enterprising attitudes demanded by employers and encouraged by many university and college courses. Under the label of 'enterprise' its associated individual attributes of initiative and independence are accompanied for many employees and self-contracting workers by growing insecurity and isolation. This is a process of proletarianisation which goes unrecognised because it is not associated with the regimentation and uniformity of the factory proletariat of the past. Indeed, it appears to follow the opposite precepts of 'creativity', 'initiative' and 'independence' – the hurrah words of the official ideology of enterprise that Prime Minister Major once promised to revive.

It is ironic that this proletarianisation of the professions is accompanied by an unprecedented expansion of the higher education with which so many professions sought to guarantee or to gain previously secure exclusive status. This expansion is not only, or even mainly, a rearguard action by the education industry to preserve its depreciated status – depreciated along with the value of its educational credentials. As has been made clear, even as their devalued currency inflates, educational credentials become increasingly important, especially to parents seeking secure, 'middle-class' status for their children, but also for anybody trying to cling on to remaining secure employment in the shrinking core of both semi-privatised public and state-subsidised private sectors. Hence the phenomenal growth in part-time, adult courses of continuing professional development, often run off-site and out of hours using distance and open learning.

The current demystification of graduate level professionalism holds teachers, doctors and other professional public servants increasingly accountable through more explicit contracts with the consumers of their previously self-regulated services. It runs concurrently with the devaluation through expansion of the major part of a more differentiated higher education system and is accompanied by the dismantling of the traditional welfare bureaucracies (including education) that have sustained the growth of the professional, or what some sociologists call 'service' class since the last world war. As has been suggested, the security of the former professions, and indeed their very claims to professional status (whether in terms of access to privileged knowledge or of self-regulation), have been increasingly undermined of late even in (what remains of) the public sector.

Students' judgements of course content and its future use in employment are obscured because the communication of generalised as well as subject specific academic or vocational knowledge in higher education is characteristically combined with the communication of a culture. For, as has also been argued, the 'brain factories' which students attend are specialised in two directions, vocational and cultural. Vocational information tends to be restricted to the job specific and technical, while less formally acquired cultural information tends to be general. It is a generalised knowledge however that, while it potentially comprehends all knowledge and, indeed, knowledge about knowledge, is not a knowledge that is socially neutral. Even in the form of the supposedly 'objective', 'scientific' knowledge of rational or logical thought, its expression is likely to be recognised, by society at large and for its hierarchies of employment in particular, as signalling superior – or traditionally middle-class – cultural status.

The balance between these two products and purposes of higher education – the cultural communication of general level knowledge combined with vocationally and subject specific information – varies with the position of particular institutions in the hierarchy of universities and colleges. We have argued that in the emerging hierarchy of competing institutions those at the top of the tree will preserve their position by selecting students from the most academic and often private schools by competitive traditional written examinations as tests in levels of literacy. Their non-vocationally specific and general courses of study, followed by students for their own intrinsic interest and in the pursuit of educational consumerism, will continue to confirm the cultural capital already acquired by students as a result of their previous upbringing and schooling. These courses function mainly as cultural apprenticeships preparing their students for positions of power and influence in society.

At the other extreme are vocationally specific courses informed with the 'personal and transferable skills' required for flexible, insecure and intermittent employment. In the colleges and former-polytechnics and in many of the older universities likely to be demoted to teaching-only (or mainly-teaching) status, students gaining access through unconventional entry requirements, or by grades in traditional examinations that show lesser levels of formal literacy, will also tend towards social similarity. The social ethos of students and institutions will thus correspond to a greater extent than previously and become mutually reinforcing. As a result, students may decreasingly share any common cultural initiation into an intellectual discourse which previously communicated generalised understanding of natural and social processes to all students in a formerly shared academic culture of higher education. Many are likely to be restricted to limited vocational information and techniques required for specific and subordinate employment.

Having established, if only in outline, at least the main social, economic and historical forces bearing upon the complex and changing system of higher education, we now go on to examine the shifting balance between the culture and content of learning in two representative universities. They are at opposite ends of the spectrum which is emerging from the expansion of further and higher education in a recession.

The Students

Let me say what student experience is not. It is not a romantic celebration of adolescence as it sometimes was in the '60s. It is something very different. (Henry Giroux, *Border Crossings*)

Home Counties University

The place

Home Counties University stands on a hill above a small cathedral town. As a 'new university' in the 1960s, it was built, like the medieval cathedral, as A.H. Halsey recorded, 'for the admiration of the peasantry without regard to their public pocket'. There is something Utopian if not monastic about the modernist buildings of the 'new universities' and indeed, they have been described as embodying 'the last fagged out gasp of the garden city movement' in architecture. Like the other 'new universities', Home Counties remains a monument to faded establishment aspirations to unite Snow's two cultures of art and science in the colleges named after the poets and scientists who were the cultural icons at the time of its foundation in 1965.

The colleges, spread about the spacious campus of woods and playing fields that they share with a large private school, represent an attempt to transplant in modern concrete and on a smaller scale a clone of Oxbridge. In this respect they resemble their academic inhabitants, many of whom moved from the antique universities in the expansion of the profession during the early 1970s that launched their careers. Such was, in Halsey's phrase, 'the grip of the ancient over the modern', that it was natural for these Oxbridge products to move from teaching the single-subject Honours degrees associated with the nineteenth century Civic universities of London and the industrial North of England, back towards the Oxbridge organisation of multi-subject schools, presenting the choice and integration of study that this allowed as a curricular innovation. Thus Home Counties, like the seven other 'new' universities built in the heyday of postwar university expansion, made, as Halsey said, 'the label they received in the 1960s meaningless'.

The 51 final-year undergraduates completing their studies who were interviewed in their last two terms at Home Counties were representative of the wider undergraduate body: mainly young 18–21 year olds moving from school to work, and from home to living away, via the transitional stage of three or four years' residential higher education – the norm for middle-class youth after the 1960s. They reflected the balance towards arts and humanities characteristic of what is basically, like the Oxbridge colleges on which it is modelled, an arts institution. They also showed the typical distribution of men and women in the sciences and information technology, where women are in the minority, as compared with the arts and social sciences where they predominate (though not among the staff).

While overseas students were not interviewed – even though many of them attend HCU, especially from other EC countries – a sprinkling of mature students across all subjects was included to reflect their participation, such as it is, at the University. Many of them live locally and, as one interviewee reported, 'the working class is well represented in the mature students'. With social commitments already established beyond the campus, mature students formed a somewhat isolated group with a distinctive attitude to their studies. As one of them stated,

> A lot of the young students treat their degree as an extension of 'A' levels, just get the books and read what they're told. The older students work a bloody sight harder than the younger ones and they worry more, try to understand what they're reading instead of just copying it out. But there again, the younger students get a hell of a lot out of it socially. They have a whale of a time – the sods!

In this respect the mature students were similar to many of the Inner City University students whose interviews are reported in the next section. Their numbers though are hardly sufficient to challenge what has been called 'the boarding school university stereotype' which Home Counties represents, and which is still echoed in the media and advertising. It is a stereotype that is under increasing pressure to change as the numbers – particularly of older students – entering higher education continue to rise.

The traditional stereotype of the typical Home Counties student persists however. Their 'apathy' was universally decried by their teachers, by many mature students and by the small minority of politically active students in the Students' Union. For example,

> None of them seem to be driven by the injustices of the system. Most of them seem to be looking after their own interests. Given that they're quite young, you'd think they'd be more idealistic. There's a great lack of energy about.

So that anyone who had expected anything different recalled their disappointment:

> I came here with a total kind of stereotype of scruffily dressed radical students and I found it wasn't anything like that. They were very much like my sixth form... They didn't give a shit and were very kind of mainstream – Marks and Spencer pullovers and Dire Straits T-shirts.

The social impression given by Home Counties University to all its students interviewed is that it is predominantly 'middle class' – even to the majority surveyed there who said that they did not themselves employ any class categorisation to make sense of their social situation. Even one of the staff with whom interviews are reported in the next chapter described it as 'a green welly university'. To those staff and students who have come from a similar educational and/or home background this is often part of the attraction of the suburban surroundings – the genteel town set in a garden-like countryside of orchards, cottages and farms.

To those who classify themselves as working class and whom it strikes as culturally foreign, this impression can be suffocating.

> There is a big difference between students here and at other universities and polies where I've visited friends. I reckon we definitely have got here a group of people, I don't know, who are pretty rich kids. There's a lot of money around. I don't know if it's maybe because it's in the South, I suppose it's inevitable the place will be more affluent. What enhances it is the way the university runs as a sort of profit-making business so the whole place is sort of money-oriented.

> They think we're all yuppies down here.

> It seems as if it's a rich university – the institution itself – and there are a lot of, well, I don't know what exactly you'd call them, but well-off

students, although obviously you get the complete spectrum as well, but they tend that way, being in the South East and close to London.

As a result and because of its small size (c.4,000 undergraduates at the time of interviews though expanding rapidly),

> It's very quiet but handy for going up to London and to the Continent [because] Poppleton is not a city for students, like the big cities, [so] the university empties out at weekends 'cos so many people come from the South and go home.

Partly because of this and because 'you can get very isolated just on campus', there is a very definite division between town and gown. Despite the best efforts of some staff and student voluntary groups,

> From my experience they're not very friendly to students. I got attacked in my first year. There was a series of attacks with this gang beating people up with iron bars and baseball bats and they went around attacking anyone who looked like a student. There are pubs in town where you're banned and there are others where locals are banned. It sounds a bit silly but apparently that's the case.

The people

A great deal of classification of self and others was evident in the student interviews and the 'snobbiness' of a minority of 'Sloaney types' was remarked upon by a number of interviewees. For example,

> You get quite a few that definitely come from a lot higher backgrounds and they go off to their winebars and places. You often spot little groups in the bar who think they're that little bit more above other people. They're all very loud and they stick to themselves.

No students interviewed actually put themselves in this reviled category of 'Sloanes' but one interviewee explained that, 'Perhaps you don't meet them 'cos at this time of year they're all off skiing or whatever.' For most students interviewed saw themselves as 'ordinary' and 'struggling' 'with money problems', so that there was, as they said, 'a mixture' of people at the university.

> A lot of them are quite posh and some of them are quite street – a range of people.

> A range – the Sloanes and the rest of us!

However, the Sloanes set the tone of the whole place, so that

> There's a lot of hidden snobbery here for no apparent reason.

Often this was based upon the schools that the students had attended previously:

> Well, in my group of friends I think ten per cent are from state schools. I don't know whether that's because I was at private school and I gravitate towards them; it's not a conscious decision.

And contrariwise,

> I don't really mix with them – public school people, people who are quite well off. They keep themselves to themselves and have money and flash clothes and that.

While others were more catholic in their acquaintance:

> I've met a lot of people who've gone to private school but then again I've met a lot of people who've gone to the same sort of school as I did.

However, as one student who grew up in a traditionally working-class locality remarked,

> Although there are a lot from comprehensive schools, they don't seem to be comprehensive schools like the one I went to.

Students also categorised themselves according to the social clubs or 'societies' that they belonged to and to an extent also these were determined by the social class of their members. For example, sport societies were reported to be 'very cliquish' and the Drama Club was especially noted for its 'loudness' and exclusivity, whereas, 'the others who are struggling to be here from working-class backgrounds tend to be very left' – often associated with the Labour Party and other groupings around the Students' Union. To an extent therefore student societies, which some interviewees admitted joining, 'just to have something on my C.V.', reproduced social gradations in the 'mixed' 'range' of students at the university.

They also overlapped with similar distinctions between students of different subjects, especially those between the minority of scientists and the rest.

> With astro-physics no one knows what you're talking about. It's a real conversation killer at a party if you tell someone that's what you study. Most people can't comprehend it. Especially the humanities. It doesn't

matter to them. We can talk about a lot of things as long as it doesn't infringe too much on their subject or my subject. Generally speaking, they don't read the same sort of books for example. Scientists read fantasy or SF. And, generally speaking, humanities students have a different view of life. They certainly have a very different attitude to their degrees. The nearest some of them get to the library is sunbathing on the grass outside! But I don't think they have an easier time. They just spend their time doing something which is quite alien to me. I mean, I think I've written three essays since I've been here, whereas they might write that many in a term. I can't put my finger on it but they're definitely different. You could say they don't have a scientific attitude. We think of problems analytically but they spend a lot of time talking about things that who's to say whether they're right or wrong. I can't see the point of it.

This mutual incomprehension was reciprocated by non-scientists:

My friends go totally around the humanities and social sciences and totally ignore the sciences; I don't know anybody who's doing science hardly. Well, some people I met in my first month whom I nod to as I pass, so I don't know if it's a typically middle-class or public school thing to do with politics. Social sciences and humanities have a lot more free time for a start and, although you very much run the risk of stereotyping in answering this question, if I was to walk into a science lecture with my ear plugs on I could tell straight away because they're just different people. I don't want to say that but they are. I don't know what the difference is because at school there was no difference and you could be doing a science and an arts 'A' level, but here they're just different people. But, there again, at school you could always tell the people who had inclinations towards science. It's not so surprising because what we sit around discussing, it's much more social, whereas what they're studying is totally alien to that and the way they apply their minds to what they apply their minds to. I think it's a real shame that even at the academic level there's absolutely no interaction between departments.

A practical reason for this disjuncture was suggested by many students:

I don't know any sociology or science students, for instance, but nobody talks to anybody. Living on campus is no different to living in town, you just get to know the people you mix with. (Humanities student)

Scientists are always out during the day and then they come back and do their work, whereas I'm in during the day but then I go out during the evening to do drama, and the people you work with there become your friends. It's just interests as well, like, I'm not into going to listen to bands and drinking a lot. Basically if you don't like drinking a lot and listening to very loud, trashy music, well you know...

A lot of scientists particularly are so into their subject that that kind of dominates their leisure time as well. The kind of people who get involved with the Students' Union tend to be social scientists and humanities. Plus the qualifications to get in for science are lower than for humanities so perhaps the social scientists feel more capable in their studies and the others feel they need to concentrate on their work.

With an intake less qualified in terms of the literary abilities assessed by 'A' level examinations and with curricula overloaded with factual information and specified practical abilities to be acquired, science and technology students could not be left by their teachers to find their own way through the books to be read and lectures to be attended to the extent that humanities and social science students could. As a humanities student put it,

I suppose one reason the scientists stick together so much is because they're in the labs so much and their courses are more set. They're plugged into their computers a lot.

While such comments indicate the organisational source of perceived differences between scientists and technologists as against the arts and social sciences/ humanities, they could also form the basis for a denigration by the predominantly arts-oriented students and staff of more rigidly structured courses for more practically oriented and less autonomous students who thus sank in the predominant hierarchy of academic prestige and esteem.

This division within the student body has been emphasised, not only because of the stereotypes of arts and science students reflected in the interviews with Home Counties students, but because it was the object of the Oxbridge-modelled college system of the University to break down such distinctions. In curricular terms, the aspiration was for higher education to be a broadening out, breaking down disciplinary distinctions and making the interconnections between them from which so many conceptual and empirical advances have been made. All students were thus supposed to have opportunities for understanding scientific, social scientific and artistic ways of looking at the world whatever their particular subject specialism. However, most students had already forsaken either science or the arts and social science two years previously when they selected their 'A' levels. That this was not subsequently corrected was due as much as anything to the organisation of their courses by academics who, it will be seen in the interviews with teaching staff, thought of themselves by and large as specialists.

Practically, students of different disciplines were mixed together in the corridors of their colleges, at least during the first term when they were supposedly guaranteed college accommodation. Actually, the college system was collapsing under the weight of increasing student numbers so that, even though all students were allocated to membership of a college not all of them could stay in it but were forced into digs and hastily built student residences. Even before this, though, the mixing of students from different faculties did not work and was regarded by many students as an artificial imposition. As one said,

> The college system shouldn't try to break you down 'cos, like my first year, I was the only humanities person on my corridor and I just had nothing in common with them [scientists].

Nevertheless, most Home Counties students followed the generally established finding that their close friends throughout college were those they met in the first few days at university. In this respect this English student was representative:

> I knew different people at different times. My close friends are those I met the first day and we all get on fine. So a reasonable cross-section but probably 80 per cent in the same sort of area as me.

Unlike the Oxbridge college system on which it was modelled, the four Home Counties colleges were not themselves the basis for divisions amongst different types of student. There were however, as one social psychology student explained, 'stereotypes of who goes to which bar' in the different colleges:

> The Sloanes and the rugby club go to one and the humanities and drama people who like to sit around and get stoned go to another and all the Union hacks go to another.

The distinctions that were signalled here were those of the social and (overlapping with them) subject and student society categories that have been noted. 'The bars are only holes in the wall anyway.'

However, it should be added that not only scientists and technologists were constrained by their more rigorous application to their subject disciplines. Humanities and social scientists, despite being left ostensibly to their own devices, were also expected to follow definite programmes of study, especially during the foundation first year when their time was taken up by a round of lectures and seminars across different subject areas. Even later, while exercising choice between the semi-modular range of option choices open to them, students were expected to remain within predefined course options. So that, as this sociologist recalled,

> I would like to have gone to more lectures in other subjects, like in literature – some authors I was interested in, but, once you get into it, it gets very inflexible. Like, I think if I went to the lecturers and said, 'Look, I'm not going to do four essays this term, only two because I'm interested in literature', they'd say, 'Bog off!'

Home Counties student perceptions of other students

At Home Counties University, student interviewees placed themselves in relation to an elite minority of Oxbridge colleges above them, and also in relation to the rest of the elaborate hierarchy of institutions that has always existed but is being defined anew in the circumstances of a market-driven expansion of higher education. On this scale, the Home Counties students are clear where they stand. This is sometimes through choice, when, as in two or three cases, they had rejected the offer of Oxbridge places in favour of the mixed degrees of less academic teaching, or because,'I didn't want to get involved in that whole thing – the balls and the boatrace'. More usually they have been relegated to what they realise is perceived as an institution of the second rank.

> This place along with Exeter and Durham, it has the reputation of picking up the cast-offs from Oxford and Cambridge and it's run on the college system so I think they try to build up the history, capitalising on the fact that a lot of people who don't get into Oxford and Cambridge come here.

> They've got to go somewhere but they couldn't quite get in there so they came here.

> Well, I certainly failed my interview for Oxford!

> We get the ones they reject!

Entry to the antique universities is therefore rationalised as either by prescription for an aristocracy or by meritocratic competition in which only the exceptionally 'gifted' gain acceptance by their effortless achievement.

> The standard procedure is you're either exceptional or with the family background to get in.

As a result,

> We haven't got the rich people who've bought their way in – the Prince of Here and the Duke of There – or people who've been nurtured into going there through the private school system.

(As a matter of historical anthropology, when it was first founded, the University operated a scheme of preferential entry for applicants whose chance of getting into their first choice, Oxbridge college was negligible but who could be persuaded to nominate Home Counties as their first choice when they would be guaranteed entry whatever their 'A' level grades – if any. Thus the University had attracted a small coterie of the Queen's cousins and other titled folk because, explained a member of staff, 'These were the kind of people we wanted to recruit and, even though this has become very much a thing of the past, the culture of it seems to live on'.)

The stereotypical impression that Home Counties interviewees had of Oxbridge students was confirmed by any students from there that they happened to meet:

> The Oxbridge students I met during merchant banking interviews were definitely higher class. They all spoke with a potato in their throat and were all shocked when they heard I came from Home Counties and not Durham or somewhere that would be a good second best to them.

> Oxford and Cambridge are notorious for snobbery and from the people I've seen there's no reason to disbelieve it.

However, Home Counties students who knew more about the ancient universities, like a former student of Ruskin, the Trades Union College in Oxford, appreciated that

> There are obviously two sides to them: there are young radicals and there are incredibly rich people. People at Oxford are less conventional than at HCU; the students – at Ruskin and the other students – have opinions and are ready to talk about them. Here they shy away from it. One of the big drawbacks of this place is you can never have a serious conversation with anyone.

So that,

The atmosphere there [at Oxbridge] is one of quite high unselfconscious academic achievement, whereas at Home Counties you sort of apologise for doing well. It's the same at polytechnics: I've got friends at Hatfield and the feeling I got was that they're all very dismissive of the academic thing.

Knowing that they were neither exceptionally gifted nor exceptionally rich, the majority of Home Counties students played down their intellectual interest and appeared often indifferent to their course of study. Their higher education was in any case something that they had been expecting and which had been expected of them by their parents and the schools to which they sent them. The exceptions here were the mature students and (as indicated, often the same thing) those from working-class backgrounds, or at least those who were amongst the first generation in their families to enter higher education. They were more likely to feel that they were lucky or even privileged to have got so far rather than to accept it as normal. This accounted for their marked enthusiasm in contrast to most of the rest of the Home Counties interviewees, who largely took their higher education for granted as the next stage in the conventional life course of middle-class youth.

There were compensations to a second-best position however, within what was still perceived by most as a privileged or fortunate student status, for the students knew (because their university teachers, and the careers advisors and schools which directed them to apply, told them so) that some subject choices are unique to Home Counties and some departments at the University enjoy superior renown to their equivalents within higher education institutions that are more highly regarded as a whole. They were also clearly aware of their superior relation to most other higher education institutions and to the former-polytechnics in particular. Here again their university lecturers and tutors must also have played a part in shaping student perceptions.

To the students, parental pressure in favour of university over polytechnic was also evident, as in

Polies are probably more with it and up to date but, having said that, my parents were adamant I wasn't going to a poly.

Home Counties students were also more or less aware (depending upon their subject of study) of employer preferences for established university graduates. For example,

> The reason I came to university rather than polytechnic was a snobbish sort of attitude on the part of employers.

This attitude had also been endorsed by their previous schools:

> Our school tended to push people into universities.

Others spoke about the 'tremendous' pressure put upon them by their schools and sometimes by their parents to get them into university.

If they had given any thought to the question of the type of student attending (former-) polytechnic rather than (longer established) university – which many Home Counties interviewees had not, answering 'don't know' to this question – they were likely to suppose, charitably, that there was no difference, that all students were the same and that such students could be distinguished only on the basis of their subjects of study. These were supposed to be more practically oriented and more vocationally relevant:

> My brother's at poly doing the same course and the whole emphasis is entirely different. Ours is sort of mathematical nonsense that no one will ever use unless you go into research but my brother's course, for a start he had a year out in industry and they don't do any of the theoretical stuff 'cos they can't see it's any use and their whole course is oriented towards employment and the other thing is they do specific courses in presentation, talking in public and things. It just seems they will be so much more adjusted to going and getting a job whereas we're, I don't know what we're set up to be, maybe just to do further research... It's to sort of stop you going out in the real world. I mean, I'm not particularly keen on getting tied down to some job so you may as well stay on here.
>
> Polies look upon us as being, like, really pampered here at university. Like my brother makes jokes about that. They look at universities as being really pretentious, calling our terms Michelmas, Lent and Trinity, things like that. It is a sort of outdated pretension and if they feed that down your throat for three years you can't help getting pretentious people out at the end of it.

Any Home Counties student who had personal knowledge of the former-polytechnic sector through visiting more than one, also knew that they, like universities, varied in their character and also by department of study within them. At the same time, many university students were also aware – either through people they knew at former-polytechnics or through knowledge of their entry requirements, even if they had not considered applying there themselves – that entry demands were generally lower. Hence,

> I get the impression people go to polies if they haven't got the brains for university rather than it being a class thing but the same sort of people.

So that,

> People who go to polytechnics are either people who didn't get good enough grades to go to university or they're people who know what they want – something practical and vocationally directed. As compared with a lot of people at university who just go there because they don't know what they want to do.

Though this could be tempered with an awareness of the social factors likely to affect these outcomes, if only at the level of the opinion:

> There's something about the word polytechnic that's very working class, as if that's where kids from comprehensives go.

Whether this perceived difference will be obscured by the unification of names or whether it will be preserved by some new label, remains to be seen.

Inner City University

The place

By contrast, many of the c.9,000 students attending Inner City University (formerly Inner City Polytechnic) full- and part-time live locally, in a world that is socially and environmentally galaxies removed, though only an hour's drive away, from the sheltered groves of Home Counties' modern academe.

> It's in a deprived area. It's not like in green country.

> There are a lot of local people at the poly, even the accountants – they're mainly Asians from round here.

But, added another student,

> I tell you what I don't see though and that is... say people in this block of flats, going to the college... I suppose what I mean is the really poor people, people who are one parent families and stuff like that.

The University, for all that it aspires to bring education to the working class, is located in an area where geographic features have produced a culture with specific economic and vocational opportunities built around the local industries. The cultural heritage of the traditional working-class majority in the area is still transmitted largely unopposed, even though the industries that created it have changed or disappeared and despite the continual settlement among the local population of a series of communities drawn originally from the former colonies of the British Empire. The dominance of this traditional working-class culture is evident in the lowest take-up rate for higher education in the country.

Here amongst the mean streets blown about with rubbish and surrounded by tower blocks, revamped docks and disused factories, our sample of fifty final year full-time students reflected the majority female and ethnic minority constitution of the student body at Inner City University. However, because they were selected from those whose term-time address was the same as their permanent address, mature students were over-represented. So were their subject choices in Independent Studies and Sociology with Professional Studies, for which conventional access requirements had often been waived. In short, they were the type of new student that the government has repeatedly said it wishes to attract to higher education. They can be contrasted with the students at Home Counties who largely conformed to the stereotypical 18–21 year-old, traditionally middle-class student.

Unlike Home Counties which is primarily an arts institution, there is at Inner City greater variety both of subjects of study, in which applied sciences and technology predominate, and of type of course (degree and non-degree). Moreover, the institution has not been static, as has HCU (until recently) since its foundation, but has been rapidly changing and expanding since its unification in 1971 from a number of discrete technical and further education colleges scattered over three separate inner city boroughs. This disparate nature of the institution, as well as its location in an urban working-class cultural community, had an effect upon its students' appreciation of their place in the unified higher education system of which both Universities now form a part.

The people

Even though,

> It's not like the most popular place to go... It's basically most people's last choice.

and

> in the prospectus it says, 'We pride ourselves on our low entrance requirements'!

for some students there, especially mature students with local domestic commitments for whom it was convenient, this openness was a virtue:

> We take them all in [so that] You don't get the snobbery at poly 'cos some students have gone to university on any course just 'cos it's a university, whereas they could've done things they wanted to at a poly.'

Mature students particularly welcomed the mixture of ages and, in contrast to Home Counties' mature students, did not feel an isolated minority. As one commented,

> The nice thing about the poly was they were so open to new ideas and encouraging to mature students.

As a result,

> It's a very good mixture

in terms of age, class and race, and this was regarded by some interviewees of all backgrounds as a source of esteem and some pride:

> Inner City must be unique for the type of student it has, not only working class, but also from very disrupted backgrounds one way and another and ICU takes them in and also all ages which you are not going to get on other courses.

For others, including the black student below, this was not such a recommendation:

> Because it's got a bad name, they attract in a lot of black and ethnic minority students and when I was applying people said, 'Oh, you'll easily get in there' and they're always boasting they've got 45 per cent ethnic minorities and the lecturers really live on that, you know, and that really pisses me off 'cos it's ironic that most of them are white.

Black and white, most students interviewed described themselves and others at the University as working class.

> On the whole the impression you'd get was that most of the students were working class, from what you hear in the canteen and so on.

> Most of the students I knew were working class.

> I would say that it took more working-class students than other university-type colleges.

> I'd say they are predominantly working class.

> I would say all of them working class.

> Mostly working class.

> 95 per cent.

As a result, there was a shared attitude to study:

> We all come from a working-class background and saw the degree as a means to the end of improving our standard of living.

Students did not take their experiences of higher education for granted as even most young students came from schools where it was not usual to progress to higher education and they were also likely to be the first in their families to continue formal study beyond school.

Like school, attendance was compulsory at Inner City – or at least, students were informed that attendance, which was registered by staff at workshops/seminars and in labs, counted towards their final assessment. Students could not therefore afford to 'take it or leave it', as some Home Counties students apparently did, though even there a system of formal registration at seminars was introduced during the course of our research. (This was disapproved of, incidentally, by those Home Counties staff for whom such procedures had previously been informal and for whom 'registering the class' smacked too much of their being a teacher, as well as detracting from the idea they had of their students as self-directed individuals, and that therefore their students had of staff, as different from their previous school teachers, as well as of themselves as students different from school pupils. See further in the next chapter.)

Also, students at Inner City could not afford to take their experience of higher education for granted, as approximately one tenth of students over all years and courses did not complete their course of study – more in some subjects. (This compares with an 'attrition rate' of c.2 per cent at Home Counties and with national 'attrition rates' over all courses of full- and part-time study of c.15 per cent. This attrition figure is for courses which currently have an age participation ratio (APR) of 20 per cent of people aged 18–21. With the APR rising to 30 per cent plus of all 18–21 year olds by the year 2000, 'attrition' can also be predicted to rise to perhaps 30 per cent also. The stigma of 'failure' may however be softened, by the development of modular schemes of study, with multiple exit and entry points – see the further discussion in chapter four.)

At Inner City during the years of our study, students were deliberately over-recruited through clearing in order to 'put bums on seats', as everyone – students and staff – said, in exchange for grant-aided funding. Thus a certain percentage were regularly and predictably failed by the institution year after year. The symbolic violence this inflicts upon students who experience this rejection as a personal failure, and feel that they have been condemned as 'thick' against objective criteria of 'intelligence' can hardly be estimated. Many mature and other students have come from educational and social backgrounds where they have already been judged as 'failures', so that this second chance represents only a second failure. This 'wastage' was highest in the first year, and compared with one or two per cent at Home Counties – though even there the old reassurances that 'nobody ever fails unless they actually don't turn up for the exam and, even then, they send someone to look for you', were no longer so certain, especially for non-standard (mature and non-'A' level) entrants.

The perception of social homogeneity which was reflected in interviews with students at Inner City varied according to course of study and site attended by the student, as these two brothers in conversation illustrate:

> It depends which group of students I'm talking about...
>
> ... It depends what course you went on as well 'cos on some courses, like the law course, everyone seems to be Nigerian.
>
> ... Yeah, for financial purposes there was a lot of foreign students on my course. The number of foreign students grew year by year because the college was, like, recruiting...
>
> ... from Malaysia.
>
> Each precinct is so different,

another student explained. For example,

> A lot of people come from a long way away to do the modular degree because it's one of the only places you can do it.

Whereas,

> The sociology course was mainly local people.

While,

> In Cultural Studies I'd say the majority were middle-class.

And,

> I think for the irregular courses – like Independent Study – as some people see them, that's the more typical working-class type of people, people who have to struggle to get where they're going, and in purely social terms Independent Study is a different ball-game altogether because they don't fit into a mould. They tend to think independently and they don't fit into what is considered normal.

As a result of this segregation,

> It was quite difficult to tell [what other students were like] because it was only in the last six months that we moved to another site and I began to see students other than sociology and Independent Studies students.

So some students could consider that the majority at Inner City were middle-class (or perhaps from what we have called the new working-middle of society), especially compared with

> the children round here in my neighbourhood... My neighbours here when you try and explain that higher education's not just a matter of getting a better job, they just don't understand.

> So the very fact that you're here means you're different... You want to get on.

There were the usual problems of definition in terms of social class, especially as, as has been remarked already and will be further considered later, it could be said that the experience of higher education made students 'middle-class' through the cultural dimension of the knowledge they acquired. In addition, there was the consideration that,

> There were an awful lot of younger people who were playing at being working-class but they always had mothers and fathers behind them when things got hard.

So many students look like they're working-class but then you find out they're just playing games.

There's a lot of middle-class students there who disguise themselves as working-class but don't really know what it means.

There's a lot of people who like to tag themselves as working class but they weren't, they just weren't, because it's almost taboo to be like known as middle-class, especially sociology students. It was mainly the sociology students that had this thing. They had the *Socialist Worker* and that sort of thing. It was amazing – you could see the transformation in them: when they came down they had the short back and sides and then, within a few weeks all that was thrown off and it was the torn jeans and all that.

'Cos I was at Tyrrell House, right in the sociology thing, everybody's known for that, being very working-class and wanting to fight and save the masses and a lot of them mature students, a lot of them would come up with the same old thing about how working-class they are and how they'll never change. But how can they say they won't change? Tyrrell House was cocooned off from the rest of the place and so everybody could come in and talk a lot about Marxism and that, which was taught there, but at Corbett the students were more right-wing...

The uniformity of opinion and type of student considered to be representative of various courses is similar to the stereotypes students at Home Counties held of each other, especially of the two cultures of arts and sciences. At Inner City however, there was greater variety of course cultures distinguished proportionately by class, gender and race. This reflected the different admissions policies or procedures of the courses. Some courses, as the students interviewed noticed, were mainly made up of one group or the other. Physiotherapy, for instance, was mainly young (18–21 year-old), white women; whereas business studies, while mainly young, was evenly divided between Asian, African/African-Caribbean and white students. Engineering students interviewed were mostly young Asian men, several from the local Tamil refugee community; and mature, African/African-Caribbean, women interviewees were concentrated in Independent Studies and sociology.

For other interviewees,

It rather depends on why they came to Inner City. If they came because they didn't make the grade for where they wanted to go they'd be middle class but if they came because of what ICP has to offer, which is quite a lot actually, then they'd be more of a mixture but you can't really tell.

The middle class there, there's lots of them but they've done badly in their 'A' levels, that's why they're there; it's a last resort. Most of the mature students are working-class.

Most interviewees, the younger ones especially, like the 18–21 year-olds interviewed at Home Counties, were not unduly conscious of social class, which seemed a subject reserved for sociology seminars.

> I think very very few, maybe 0.1 per cent think of themselves as middle-class and everybody else doesn't really seem very conscious of class. It's very integrated like that.

> It's a real mixture but I don't know what I'm looking at when I'm thinking of that – What their parents do? Yes that's what I'm looking at but you can't really judge if they're professional people or not, but that's the sort of question that's never asked anyway; they're just your friends.

Thirty years ago, interviewing Parisian students before the 1968 May events which his classic study of students predicted, Pierre Bourdieu noticed

> students generally evade the simple naming of their parents' occupation, whatever it may be. Their embarrassed silence, half-truths, or declared dissociation are all ways of distancing themselves from the unacceptable idea that such an unchosen determination could determine the choices of someone entirely occupied in choosing what he or she is to be.

Thus, Bourdieu argued, students actively engage with and sustain the notion of equality of opportunity for meritocratic selection which higher education supposedly offers them.

Inner City student perceptions of other students

As seen, the students at Inner City found it less easy to categorise their institution as uniformly as those at Home Counties. This is both because of the greater variety of type of course (degree and non-degree) within it and because the situation there is and always has been more fluid. The predominant social (and racial/national, as well as class, gender and age) characteristics of the students depends, as has been indicated, upon the course that they are following. One part of the split site thus differs markedly from another, and not all students (or staff) necessarily visit all parts of the campus. Again, some departments enjoy a national, even international, reputation and others are of a unique character, both of which factors draw students who are not local. Of those who are, several also come from adjacent suburban areas and from families and schools (whether state or private) which have given them aspirations to attend a longer established university rather than a former-polytechnic. Therefore several former-polytechnic students also have a clear perception of their position in the educational and consequent employment hierarchy. As one particularly despondent interviewee put it, 'Let's face it, nobody comes to Inner City unless they're desperate!'

However, as with the Home Counties students in relation to the colleges they know are ranked above them, Inner City students appreciated that their degree courses are worth as much if not more in terms of course content as the same courses at university. This was also emphasised to them by their lecturers, one of whom reportedly told his students, 'The polies are the poor man's universities'. The same lecturer also explained to his students that they would be expected to work harder for the same degree qualification because they had typically entered their course of study at a lower starting point – two, instead of three, low grade, instead of high grade, 'A' levels, or with other entry qualifications such as BTEC or City and Guilds, or by access routes or sometimes with no formal qualifications at all. Their final degree qualifications would however be of equal worth, even if former-polytechnic students knew that they would not be regarded as such by employers. As one Inner City interviewee explained the difference between established university and former-polytechnic, 'It's a bit like grammar and comprehensive but you can get the same qualification in both places'. Indeed, this was recognised by many students and staff at Home Counties University and not only when they are speaking in 'enlightened' or patronising mode.

The Inner City University students pick up their perception of their place at the bottom of the hierarchy from their teachers, from any comparison they are able to make with university students on the same courses and from the amount of work they are asked to undertake in order to reach the same level from a 'lower' starting point. These signals can be confirmed by careers officers, as related by one interviewee:

> I didn't get much confidence exuding from the Careers Service since they told us that as mature graduates from Inner City you're down the

bottom of the list and the only thing that's open to you is teacher training.

Employers also:

None of the firms bother to come here at the milk-round, just the odd government department.

This estimation may well be reinforced by the changing of the names, as well as by those shadows of the traditional university experience which percolate down to Inner City and its largest site (recently redesignated campus), where new residential blocks for the typical school-leaving student it now aims to attract are being rapidly built. For these mainstream students, their experience of higher education at Inner City University will therefore come closer to that of students at HCU, with similar societies and social activities, just as that at Home Counties shadows, though more closely through deliberate organisation, the collegiate experience of Oxford and Cambridge that is contiguous with that of the elite private schools.

What students learn and how they learn it

Although they spent less time in formal study, Home Counties students reported that they learnt more than the Inner City students who were more intensively taught. This was because, being by and large younger, Home Counties students knew less to start with and learnt more 'just as a result of growing up', 'living away from home', 'coping', 'learning to live with people my own age', so that 'I've become more tolerant' or 'I'm not so shy' and 'I can cook now!' As one of them summarised: 'It's the social thing that's most valuable about coming here – living away from home with a group of people, getting on with them – social development.' Students also acquired social skills through involvement in societies, on course committees and through the Students' Union, which Inner City students were less likely to do because many of them lived at home and because societies and college social events played less of a part in student life generally.

Interviewees at both institutions considered their social skills had also been improved by seminars (or workshops, as they were called at Inner City), particularly their skills of presentation, but some did not think they had acquired anything 'just by sitting in seminars and arguing'. A few even considered that they had become more antisocial as a result of their study because

> You're very much alone in the library doing essays (Home Counties English student)

and

> The course doesn't promote talking to people; it promotes sitting at terminals. So if you're a shy sort of person you could become very introverted (Home Counties Information Technology student).

Such people were known as 'terminal termites'.

The competitive and individual ethos of study was also commented on by some Inner City students who had not anticipated it but seemed to be taken for granted by most Home Counties interviewees. However, several Inner City (but very few Home Counties) students had studied collectively, either on their own initiative or because teamwork was built into the structure of their courses, especially Independent Study.

Mature students at Home Counties, like those who made up the majority of the sample at Inner City, felt that they already had the social skills that younger students valued acquiring:

> I wasn't a wilting wallflower before I went to college.

> I'd worked for ten years already.

> I hadn't just left school so I knew about work, about organising my time and working with people.

> Anyone who's been a housewife can organise their time.

Subject of study was considered irrelevant to what most Home Counties students thought they had learnt at university. For them, the main benefits of their three or four years of study came from 'meeting people', 'being in the artificial environment of so many like minds', 'just being with 4,000 other students in a relaxed atmosphere'. Though this opinion was tempered by the awareness that, 'You mostly meet people from the same background so you don't get challenged except in terms of ideas'. And its artificiality in terms of age was commented on by a mature student who said that, with so many young people around, 'It's like a rock festival with no music'.

Inner City students were more likely to feel that their courses of study were vocationally relevant. They particularly valued work placements and the projects that they had undertaken on them, whereas for Home Counties students specific options in their courses, especially including individual project work, and years abroad, were held in equivalent regard.

Home Counties students had a clearer perception of the traditional academic disciplines of their courses, even if they had combined them, than the more loosely defined mixed and modular degree courses at Inner City. Indeed the whole point of Independent Study at the former-polytechnic was that it enabled study to degree level outwith any predefined subject area (see chapter four).

While equal numbers of former-polytechnic and longer established university students stated that they had acquired technical skills, more Home Counties students than Inner City students reckoned they had acquired written language skills, but fewer had acquired computing skills, including word-processing. They were more likely to consider their courses 'impractical', 'irrelevant', 'too theoretical' and 'abstract'. More also expressed negative attitudes towards new technology than the Inner City students interviewed. This was especially marked for social science students, many more of whom at Inner City had practised statistical analyses than had their Home Counties counterparts for most of whom computers remained an unknown quantity so that, as one said, 'Computers mystify me completely.'

Courses at Home Counties that attempted to compensate for this 'techno-phobia' were regarded as 'poorly organised', 'half-hearted' and 'irrelevant'. For example,

> Computing for anthropology taught me what I thought I knew already – that I didn't like computers and I didn't get on with them.

This was a minority experience at Inner City, though many students there admitted to hard struggles before they came to 'get on with' new technology. Similarly, more of all the Inner City students had access to and used word-processors than Home Counties students. Nevertheless this did not stop the Home Counties student quoted above intending to do an MA in computing and anthropology, 'because I think it's a very important skill to have in our society'! Nor a theology student from gaining a job in computer consultancy on the basis of a three-week summer course, even though she had no previous experience of computing and considered that

The one thing I was really pleased I learnt at university was how to write references with '*ibid.*' and '*op. cit.*' and all that.

'Confidence' was what many students felt they had gained from their higher education and 'confidence', as has been said, 'breeds competence'. To student interviewees of working-class origin, the power which education conferred was more immediately apparent than to those who already took it for granted. It was apprehended as a growth in confidence that was expressed in the most enthusiastic terms.

> It was almost like a religious experience, going from working in a factory and being unemployed to be told you can get to university. I thought they were taking the piss quite honestly. I just looked on it as a year away from work and then the confidence just sort of hits you as you're going through it and people are starting to take you seriously as a thinking person – lecturers and qualified professional people.

As a result mature students (over 25) at HCU were the most markedly enthusiastic of any interviewees about their studies. 'Quite transformed – sleepers awake – scales from the eyes, any cliché you like,' was a typical evaluation. At Inner City mature students had often made such efforts to combine demanding home lives with full-time study that, while they were often appreciative of the transformative experience of their higher education, they could not afford to be so enthusiastic about it. However, mature students at both institutions were most likely to express an intention to continue with study, as they had now 'caught the studying bug', as more than one of them put it. More Inner City interviewees (more of whom were mature) spontaneously mentioned a growth in confidence as a result of their study than did Home Counties students for whom confidence was a result of gaining maturity and independence. This was particularly the case for female Home Counties students.

For the younger Home Counties students, further study, if unnecessary for their future careers, was regarded as a fall-back in face of unemployment, an academic future not being rated very highly in career terms. This was not the case amongst Inner City students, for whom academic teaching or research was seen as an ideal if perhaps also unobtainable occupation. They were at once more appreciative of their lecturers' efforts to help them and more critical of any failings to do so than were the Home Counties students interviewed, though among both it was a general opinion that most teaching staff were more interested in their own research than anything else.

Both groups of students considered their vocabulary had been enhanced by their higher education, though more Home Counties students stated that they had developed their written communication ('writing essays') while Inner City students stressed oral communication – 'You speak differently without realising it.' Other people could realise it though:

> I lost a lot of friends. They couldn't adjust to me. My personality sort of changed and they started calling me a yuppy but I hadn't changed. I just used a wider vocabulary but I didn't do it deliberately. It was just I was writing so many essays and the dictionary must've been red-hot the amount I was using it and then I started coming out with these things.

More Inner City interviewees felt that they now 'thought differently' as a result of their studies, especially about issues of race, gender and politics which often affected them personally and which had been emphasised on their courses. But both groups of students agreed that it was their cognitive, analytic or problem-solving capacities that had benefitted most from their studies.

Comparing cognitive content

However this was defined, general level cognitive content – what has been called here generalised as opposed to more limited, vocational knowledge and skill, 'the ability to learn how to learn' valued by the official pronouncements of employers, or the 'underpinning knowledge' necessary to supplement technical competence as supposedly measured for instance by General National Vocational Qualifications – would seem to be the real acquisition of higher education in both institutions. Despite pedagogical differences, interviewees at both institutions in all subjects and modes of study estimated that their higher education had provided them with capabilities of a general and analytic kind, rather than with specific vocational or technical skills (though often these had been acquired as well).

This was particularly appreciated by students of working-class origin in contrast with their previous experience:

> I had such narrow views before [and] you think you know everything with just a little knowledge. [But now,] nothing is cut and dried any-

more. Everything leads to a further question. I can never find an answer to anything. It's always 'But', 'What if?', 'On the other hand'. There's always more to find out. There's so many ways of looking at it. [So,] you never take anything at face value any more. You just question things. You don't accept anything maybe in the way you once did. More open-minded I should imagine. That comes through all the discussions you have, finding out about things historically and how things come about. There's nothing new in this world; it's all happened before.

As a result,

'You become more critical', 'detached', 'analytical', 'open-minded', [leading to] 'a broader view of the world' [in which] 'I look at more issues now', 'objectively' [and] 'from different points of view' – 'a logical way of looking at things'.

There are always exceptions to the rules. I think you become aware of that in higher education more than anything else.

In part, 'an ability to see all sides of an argument' and to 'solve problems' was felt to have been acquired in all subjects at both institutions. Most felt that three or four years of study had given them, if not an expertise, then overall familiarity with a given area, even if this was sometimes narrowly defined by traditional academic boundaries. Most interviewees agreed that the principles of understanding in their particular discipline were applicable in general form to the intellectual comprehension of related and other areas. For example,

I think with physics you don't really change the way you think because it's a specialised area that you've already been introduced to and you just think, "how do the laws of physics apply and can what I know of maths apply to that?" – I even do it when I'm watching telly.

And similarly,

The main skill of history is being able to take a large and incoherent body of information and put it into a coherent presentation, turning it into something understandable. I don't think it's a particularly tangible skill. I suppose by that I mean it's nothing directly employable.

Or, as another Home Counties' student stated,

Really it's how to handle information rather than the information itself.

Generalised knowledge in this sense, and as defined in chapter one, of understanding the rules by which to order information, rather than the acquisition of information itself, or of more or less vocationally specific techniques and competences was recognised by interviewees as an outcome of their higher education. But some of them restricted this 'general knowledge' to an understanding of general relations within their particular discipline or subject of study. Thus, a number of Home Counties scientists, noticeably, disclaimed any knowledge of politics and social questions in particular, leaving that to others who had 'specialised' in those areas. Reciprocally, Home Counties humanities and social science graduates professed ignorance of scientific specialisms and – particularly in the arts – of the general processes of scientific thinking.

In part, this indicated a positive self-identification with their subject discipline (an identification which it will be seen in the staff interviewees in the next chapter was important for staff self-image and their contrasted orientations to pedagogic issues). It was less the case at Inner City, where more interviewees had followed mixed modular and Independent Study degrees across or beyond discipline boundaries, and where interviewees were more generally opinionated whatever their subject of study. This closed attitude was however also evident among particular social science disciplines at Home Counties. For example, an economist there declined to answer the interview questions on politics 'because it's not my subject', and would not commit himself to an opinion even on questions of Britain's economic future 'because it's so complicated' and 'I would need a few sides of A4 to explain it properly'. (Such attitudes were mirrored in some staff interviewed at Home Counties. For example, the historian who declined to be interviewed about the contemporary situation of higher education because 'That is a question which will be decided by the historians of the future'!) For a minority of interviewees, therefore, general level thinking skills were not opened to other areas where they could have been applied, but deliberately restricted to the particular area of their acquisition.

In his classic formulation of the liberal idea of a university Cardinal Newman declared that 'not to know the relative disposition of things is the state of slaves and children', and, he could have added, of the majority of the working class of his day. Yet working-class (or any) individuals can acquire such an overall view, and the same generalised knowledge and analytic abilities of rational or scientific thinking, by their own efforts, without attending higher (or any) education, though it may be hard for them to do so. It is just that such forms of generalised knowledge and ways of thinking are likely to be recognised by others as typical of the 'middle' rather than 'working' class and can therefore be deployed, along with the badges of qualification attesting to their formal certification, as marks of 'Distinction' to gain entry to typically 'middle-class' occupations and society, or just reasonably secure and better remunerated 'core' posts with prospects of career progression from which others are increasingly excluded.

If scientific, logical, deductive thinking, which can be applied in a variety of situations, is distinguishable from the predominant ideology or culture of a class also communicated by traditional higher education, it must rest in such elite higher education institutions upon foundations of tacit knowing acquired either directly through technical or cultural apprenticeship or indirectly by reading in the disciplines of science or the humanities. As such, it may or may not be common to the distinct cultures of different courses that are a product of admissions procedures, staff attitudes, and, crucially, the intrinsic, cognitive status of curriculum content by which the dispositions of individual applicants, curriculum content, and institutional ethos are moulded together to constitute the marketable commodity of students graduating to particular employments.

We have argued however, that such generalised knowledge and skills were shown by our interviews to have been shared by graduates of Inner City as well as Home Counties, whatever the social polarities between them. In other words, there was at the time of our interviews among the students whom we interviewed at the completion of their courses an academic culture of higher education shared by both institutions and the various courses of study within them.

For Home Counties students this cognitive content was again,

> Partly because you're getting older – you think more logically and don't, like, rush in so fast.

But it was also much more than this, as expressed most cogently by a film studies student:

> I've come to understand more how the world around us is constructed ideologically rather than taken for granted... Nothing is the way it seems. Everything is constructed for some reason by some agency... I've got no particular interest in films; it just seems that's the only area

where people have started to explore these ideas. You need to talk about something...

This is a knowledge that knows and can justify the basis of its own knowing. Without falling into the cultural relativism that asserts that all knowledge is socially constructed, so that no reality can ever be apprehended or expressed beyond the emptiness of endless language games, this student saw his subject – which, as he said, was irrelevant – as a social product rather than as an embodiment of absolute standards and values. His belief that nothing was so certain could be carried over to question other received ideas and behaviours. Their ultimate test would therefore become that of reality itself, against which criterion truth might be distinguished from ideology.

This ability to talk and to think at such a level is clearly entangled with cultural attitudes which were difficult for interviewees to distinguish in retrospect if only because, as a Home Counties student stated,

It's difficult to think back to before... it's hard to separate what you knew before from what you learnt.

This was also because interviewees felt they had done such a lot in such a short time. It was thus difficult to take stock so that, as an Inner City student said,

I don't think you realise it so much as you're going through. When you hear first years worrying about their work and you find yourself advising them and when you look back on your first year essays you just want to curl up and die!

The end result was

...a loss of innocence really. Books were just books before. [Now] it's very hard to watch plays or read books without this other analysis going on in your head... I think a lot differently. You sort of see things in a different light once you go into them.

Consequently, higher education had given students of working-class origins a choice. Like the heroine of *Educating Rita*, a mature Inner City student explained,

You think differently and you speak differently without realising it. You can go either way now. You can go with people like the people we used to go around with – you can come down to their level, but you can also go up a level, to talk to people about their subject and understand it.

And another added,

> There's one thing I must mention about higher education: once you've experienced it, it seems to open a lot of areas you've never thought about; it seems to show you that there are different ways of being satisfied in your life, because now I've thought to myself that whatever job I do I can enjoy, following my own interests and reading and doing other things.

> Once you've studied the world becomes a smaller place and you tend to look at people as more a single society. You begin to find common values between individuals.

> You can talk to anyone.

How much they would subsequently be able to exercise this choice in the occupations open to them depended upon the labour market to which their higher education gave them access, as well as to the support networks which, if they did not already exist, they had managed to build up at college. In this connection, Home Counties interviewees more often mentioned among the benefits of their higher education the importance of partnerships and other relationships with fellow students, particularly friendships, that they had made and intended to maintain after graduating. This was less the case at Inner City, even though, as seen, interviewees there reported less individual competition and more collaborative working than Home Counties students.

Being older and local, Inner City students already had, as mentioned, social lives outwith the institution, though sometimes these were uncomprehending of if not in conflict with it. For instance,

> Something a lot of us [mature students] have noticed is, you know, family and friends they don't know what you're doing. They think it's a little part-time course to get you out of the house. Like a friend of mine stunned me the other day; she asked me, 'What is a degree?'. You know, that really amazed me because she's really interested in education for her children; you know – private tutor coming in and everything, and she hadn't got a clue. And going to a poly and not a university, people think degrees only come from universities and polies are only for evening classes.

How far such students' previously established social identities conflicted with their new potential roles and caused them to revert to their previous social state after they left college also relates to how much real – as opposed to only potential – choice was available to them after graduation. Certainly several contrasted their previous lives with their future intentions, for example:

> I'll be looking towards progressing, whereas before I really didn't care at all because of my family circumstances, because I put them first, so I never wanted to commit myself.

Inner City students were particularly aware of the transformation that had occurred to their thinking at least, as illustrated by two brothers in conversation:

> You always have to doubt things... You want to know why...
>
> ... To counter arguments before you say things... you become more, like, argumentative...
>
> ... Well, more opinionated...
>
> ... More objective...
>
> ... Pessimistic...
>
> ... Cynical.

Or, as another Inner City student speculated, 'more middle-class'.

Class cultural content

In part their study was seen by students from working-class backgrounds at both institutions as a cultural apprenticeship:

> It was a really good course for introducing you to names that are always bandied about by people – Marx and Freud and people – and unless you study them I felt I would never get any understanding of what they were on about and I kind of feel now that I've got the confidence to go further if I wanted to, whereas if I hadn't studied them on my course I wouldn't dream of picking up one of their books.

Students of working-class origin at Home Counties had also acquired what they saw as middle-class habits:

> like nice food and going to the opera and reading, which my parents would say was dead snobby, or just, saying 'lunch' and 'dinner' instead of 'dinner' and 'tea'.

So that, as one Home Counties University student put it, whatever class students originally came from, 'They'll be middle-class by the time they leave here!'

The notion of studenthood as a cultural apprenticeship relates to the vexed question of students' class of destination – whether, whatever their class of origin, the higher education process made them, as many interviewees said that it did, 'middle-class'. Although,

> We had a discussion about this last week and we came to the conclusion that education takes you out of the working class but that doesn't mean you're middle-class, so you don't know where you are in the end.

As compared with,

> Well, my background I would think of as working-class but myself, because I've gone through the education system, I wouldn't expect to go into what I would consider working-class occupations, for example shop assistant, so I don't really consider myself in a class at the moment but I don't really think about it.

Or,

> Now I would say I was working-class but people I was at school with wouldn't agree with me. I was brought up on a council estate in a posh area so all my friends were middle-class and they all think they've slipped back in comparison with me. They'd like to think they're working-class.

So,

> I would like to be classless but everybody thinks about it so much I've got to the point where I think I'm me and that's it.

And,

> I came out of a working-class background and I don't know what I am now.

Certainly at Home Counties,

> University changes you; you couldn't not change after three years in an elitist middle-class institution. In a way I've come to accept it but that's the extent of it. I still find wine bars like obnoxious places. I don't think I've kind of taken on this middle-class kind of culture. That was something else that was alien to me. I'd been to a restaurant a couple of times in my life before I came here. Especially the first year when you don't want to miss out, I spent far too much money in restaurants. Transport – I've acquired this horrible middle-class habit of taking taxis and getting into debt – an overdraft, but it's all figures; it just doesn't mean that much. I remember I was extremely worried the first time I

had, like, £200 overdrawn but now I don't worry. I've been given a £2000 limit... to a certain extent there's a culture of people who don't want to be in debt – like, if my parents knew about my overdraft. I still resent being called a snob because I've been to university. They think you must've been privileged to get there. The same thing as I faced from working-class kids on the council estate when I went into sixth form.

I've got a lot of middle-class culture which I used to feel dead guilty about but I don't any more 'cos it's better than what they give the working class... That was the reason I left home 'cos my parents wanted me to go to work. I've got the view that I'm going to enjoy myself while I'm here and I don't see why I should sit at home and be miserable. I've got, like, a really middle-class attitude to money now. To be in debt like this five years ago would've completely spaced me out – I'd've been on drugs! Now I think, 'Sod it!'

This question of which class students belong to and whether higher education makes or confirms them as 'middle-class', wherever they come from, has been as widely debated by sociologists as, to judge from the responses of student interviewees like that above, it apparently is by students themselves, especially sociology students!

The lecturers say you're middle-class – we've discussed this endlessly in seminars.

This was despite the fact that many interviewees, especially those at Home Counties, eschewed the notion of any categorisation of self or others in terms of social class to make sense of their situation. Answers given to this question by interviewees and by sociologists vary from the simple 'By definition all students are middle-class' (mature Inner City student), to Erik Olin Wright's ambivalent neo-Marxist notion of certain statuses, such as those occupied by higher education students, having 'contradictory class locations' in which individuals share attributes of the classes above and below them and from which they may transfer either upwards or downwards.

The difficulty of classifying students by the usual occupational indices arises from the fact that students have no occupation as such, since most courses – save the most specifically vocational (law, accountancy, medicine, architecture, etc.) – do not relate to definite occupational outcomes but have general relevance to a range of possible outcomes. A student's occupation in the majority of cases is therefore, as has been said, merely to prepare for an as yet unspecified occupation.

To an Inner City student the rite of passage higher education had afforded him was palpable in the work he had begun even before graduation as a non-manual, social worker instead of (as before) a manual worker:

> I've learnt the power of education and how you can exclude people and how as soon as you mention a degree you can shut a lot of people up and people will listen to you 'cos in this job I have to deal with doctors to get prescriptions for people on heroin and so on. I mean, the last doctor I was dealing with she asked me, 'Have you got the qualifications to do this job?' and I said, 'Yeah, I've got a degree' and then she would talk to me like... And another thing it's taught me is that you can bullshit people with education, you can talk a lot of nonsense. It's power, you know. You can even make things up and they'll still believe you. There's a tremendous amount of power, you know.

The real 'personal and transferable skills'

At the middle management level, for which higher education generally prepares its students, the same demands are being made nowadays as of the workforce lower down – less for the specific vocational competences acquired within particular companies and other organisations and more for so-called 'personal, transferable skills'. These are actually general or universal competences required in a variety of work situations rendered increasingly identical by the similar use of information technology and similar new forms of work organisation (contracting, adaptability, team-working on focused problem-solving, in the 'flattened hierarchies' of the new 'flexible firm'). Unlike general level knowledge and the real skills represented by that knowledge in action, the new generic competences, and the bits of information that are their counterpart at this more limited level of learning, are closed at a lower level of understanding than general level knowledge/skill. Their performance does not lead on, as does general knowledge/skill, to questioning and justifying the purpose of the activity for which they are employed.

As has been seen, it is the informal curriculum of campus and college activities that teaches students most of the lessons that they learn at university, beyond the often specialised and limited technical competence or factual information about their particular subject of study. This is why young Home Counties student interviewees learnt more even though they studied less, whereas mature and Inner City students living at home studied more but learnt less – partly because they knew more to start with. The absence of such extra-curricular activities at the former-polytechnics and elsewhere is compensated for by the addition of 'skills' courses to the formal curriculum. So-called 'personal transferable skills' are then taught separately from the culture of which they form a part. Yet they are neither personal, transferable, nor skills; they are social and generic competences.

Generic – not transferable – competences are required in a variety of work situations, which the latest applications of new technology are rendering increasingly similar. This is the new vocational competence and information that is demanded for what were formerly distinct employments selecting employees for specialised occupations. Such competences as teamworking, familiarity with information technology and with the main European languages are becoming integrated with subject teaching across the separate discipline cultures of higher education. These competences are taught as means to ends rather than as subjects of knowledge/skill in their own right, save for those who specialise in them for such disciplines as languages or computer studies. Where previously separate and self-sufficient subjects of study are combined, through modularity for example, the part played by various competences tends to be greater.

But the effort to acquire other social, generic competences – not 'personal, transferable skills' – by formal teaching rather than as part of the culture of the informal curriculum of college and campus, could result in the opposite to the intended effect. To present attitudes and habits detached from their cultural context as technical abilities that can be acquired piecemeal in performance not only divorces them from the cultural context that gave them their original meaning but represents them as equally accessible to all students whatever their class cultural background, gender or race. It ignores the fact that middle-class students already possess many of these competences as a result of their previous education and family socialisation. As Bourdieu pointed out, even if middle-class students do not already have all of these social abilities, their previous experience lays the foundations on which to build them. The attempt to formulate explicitly this tacit information communicated by cultural practice for formal learning can thus be self-defeating and may only make students self-conscious of their failure to attain an impossible performance. By contrast, those who already possess these qualities possess also a confidence, the acquisition of which through higher education was valued by many interviewees who did not initially possess such qualities. Their educational experience had thus legitimated not only the knowledge they had acquired but legitimated also their change of status.

For at rock bottom the real 'personal and transferable skills' required for preferential employment are those of whiteness, maleness and traditional middle-classness. These are the really generic social competences that are the most acceptable to most employers. A flick through a few graduate brochures will indeed confirm this impression. No self-declared 'equal opportunities organisation' will of course admit that they are after the same 'chaps like us' as they always have been. Nor that, with the over-supply of graduates and the inflation in their qualifications, for a dwindling supply of secure career posts, new demands for 'personal transferable skills' are being added to job specifications as a way of further screening candidates. Unlike examination marks, these personal qualities are judged informally by employers who share the same inexplicit competences and information derived from a common cultural background. Similarly, large employing organisations use experts in psychometric testing and 'biodata' as ways of screening applicants, even down to issuing dauntingly long and complex application forms as disincentives for all but the most persistent applicants. Again, work placements can be used as extended interviews.

Although much of the study at Inner City University was practical and work-oriented compared with the theoretical emphasis of many Home Counties University courses, more university than former-polytechnic students expressed attitudes associated with the values of 'enterprise' encouraged, for instance, by the Department of Employment sponsored Enterprise in Higher Education Initiative. This sought to encourage entrepreneurial and work-related changes in the academic curriculum. Whether or not they were involved in 'enterprise' projects at HCU, most students there were confident enough to be quite enterprising already. Many were prepared to take risks to achieve entrepreneurial success and often aspired to direct their own companies. One interviewee while studying even ran a small off-shore oil business employing six men in the Netherlands.

By comparison, in some cases among the working-class and/or mature students at Home Counties, as well as at Inner City, predominant attitudes confirmed a lack of confidence that still mentally hobbled even those who had overcome severe disadvantages to achieve good degree passes. For example, one mature Inner City graduate of new technology made redundant from a job that he had done since leaving school and which he had felt 'comfortable in' even though it was, as he described it, a 'junior management' job, 'just making sure that the day to day administration is complied with', compared his situation then with that now he had just graduated:

> Now with the degree I look through the adverts every week and I don't know what I'm going to do and also I don't feel as confident now as I did before. Yes, I feel less confident now. I think that's the basic thing with me anyway, my confidence... I've really got no confidence. It's more than my school experience; it's my home life because I had a very unhappy childhood.

Higher education had not legitimated any change in this student's status, nor did he feel 'confident' about it, because his situation was the same, or even worse, than before he started studying. Such a condition may become more widely shared in a situation of 'education without jobs'.

Lecturers, tutors and other staff therefore have to be very careful what they say in relation to the often fragile confidence of the students they deal with daily, whose lives they can influence through what they say to them. For example, one mature, black woman student at Inner City mentioned what was perhaps a chance or off-hand remark by a lecturer that she had taken to heart and which confirmed her own low opinion of herself:

> One the lecturers said, 'You're not management material really' and that's stuck in my mind.

As a result,

> I can't see myself standing up in front of a conference of people and talking to them but maybe I should.

Often recognising 'The Hidden Injuries of Class' as a result of childhood and schooling did not necessarily make them easier to overcome and, despite the help they reported they had received, many mature students at Inner City laboured under severe personal difficulties – bringing up children single-handed, disability, financial problems – including eviction in one case and homelessness in another. These hampered their efforts both to enter and complete their courses and, as mentioned above, necessarily coloured their learning experience. As a result many of them found their courses more demanding than they had anticipated, whereas most HCU students found them less demanding.

Skin colour, gender, age and accent were impossible to change. Indeed, students at both institutions were sceptical about the equal opportunities supposedly open to them in employment. Women and black students considered that they would have to be at least twice as good to get the same job as a white male applicant. Even white, male Home Counties students knew, often from personal experience of interviews for jobs in the City of London and for merchant banking, that they would take second place to the Oxbridge and public school 'old boy net'. At Inner City, a graduate of estate management recalled:

> I went for a job to Saville's – it's like a top property firm – and they wanted to know, like what your father does and what type of school you went to. They just want to know if you went to a public school or a comprehensive, state school. He didn't say, 'What school did you go to?' He said, 'What type of school did you go to?'

As a result,

> People on my course who went to public school they had so many job interviews and if you went to a comprehensive like hardly no one got a job interview and, I mean, their grades over the three years they were just average, like 50 per cent, and their 'A' level grades were poor but they seemed to get more interviews. That's the facts.

3

The Staff

Academic persons, when they carry on study, not only in youth as
a part of education, but as the pursuit of their maturer years...
become decidedly odd not to say rotten and those who may be
considered the best of them are made useless to the world by their
study. (Plato, *Republic*, Book VI)

Two models of higher education

Twenty teaching staff at the two universities were interviewed, to
place in perspective the student experiences summarised in the
last chapter. They represented all levels from lecturer to professor
in the very different managerial structures of the two institutions,
which at Home Counties, as explained, tends to the collegial
Oxbridge model of donnish democracy in comparison with the
more centralised hierarchy at Inner City. At both places however,
it was the shop-floor lecturer who was the target of investigation,
as being representative of the reality of the situation on the ground
and its likely future development, rather than the official institutional rhetoric of 'mission statements' and glossy brochures. Staff
have opinions on this longer term future of their institution, to
which they are committed more or less enthusiastically, and these
options are not always evident to students who usually remain
within the institution for only three or four years, so that, as is
often said by staff, students come and go but the institution lives
on.

The Oxbridge background of staff at Home Counties, which
has already been commented on, was evident in this sample; all
except one of the interviewees in humanities and social science
had previously studied as under- or post-graduates at Oxbridge.
This was not the case with the Home Counties science staff interviewed nor with any of the staff interviewed at Inner City.

It is less the case at Home Counties, with its importation of Oxbridge staff, but generally within the profession a normal career path has become established in which lecturers serve an apprenticeship at a (former-)polytechnic before moving on to one of the older universities. If they manage to go straight into a university post, they must regard themselves and are regarded as fortunate and/or talented. Those left behind in the former-polytechnics or present college sector must therefore feel somewhat demoralised, unless they are particularly committed. Similarly, those parachuted in from Oxbridge to rise rapidly through the ranks are resented by other university staff who have made the normal more arduous progress.

Though it was not shared by a small minority of the Oxbridge-educated staff, one of two contrasted conceptions of higher education, and of the nature of their subject discipline within it, could be identified with the traditional university ideal that is symbolised by Oxford and Cambridge. This view sees university education as a conversation restricted to academic peers into which students are initiated and by which general and analytic knowledge is handed down, essentially unchanged, from don to potential don. This task of academic vocational education is regarded by its proponents as a vital task, literally, to the preservation of civilisation as they know it, and one that in the present economic and political climate is increasingly beleaguered on all sides.

In this view higher education is seen as building upon students' previous schooling, or, exceptionally, college education or even training in work, but is considered to differ fundamentally from them. Other university students (than potential dons) may incidentally benefit from a higher education so conceived, but the university is not essentially concerned with them, even though only eight per cent of graduates go on to further study, according to the Association of Graduate Careers Advisory Services in 1992. Similarly but also incidentally, it was considered in this view that the wider society may also possibly benefit from the free enquiry, scholarship and research which is seen as vital to advance, through gradual and organic accretion of the canon of texts or cases making up fixed subject-based knowledge. Communicating this canon either to students or a wider public is however not understood to be the essential purpose of a university, any more than are the practical applications of new ideas and the discoveries of research.

This academic ideal is, as has been said, based on the idea of knowledge for itself rather than knowledge for a purpose. Instead, the essential function of a university is, as the founder of educational sociology, Emile Durkheim, described it (in *History of Pedagogy in France*, first published in 1928) 'for an organised body of professional teachers to provide for its own perpetuation'. An individual's commitment in this conception is thus, as one interviewee related, 'to research, to my subject, to my colleagues primarily.'

The other model of education, subscribed to by an overall minority of the staff interviewed, corresponds with what we have posited as the original notion of polytechnic education – though (see p. 5), only partially embodied in the polytechnics as they developed from 1965 to 1992. This model was not held by all the staff interviewed at Inner City, though a majority of them subscribed to it, just as a minority of Home Counties interviewees also did. In addition, there was, as would be expected, a mixture of the two views sustained by many individuals in different varying proportions. Some interviewees might also subscribe to 'soft' positions themselves but be regarded as 'hard' by colleagues; for instance, an Inner City lecturer who organised classes to help students with essay writing – a typically 'soft' activity, but who had also succeeded in gaining some 'hard' research funding for herself. The two polarities of the contrasted conceptions can thus be regarded as 'ideal typical' models, deriving from the equally 'ideally typified' scheme of the development of higher education in Western Europe outlined in chapter one.

This second conception of higher education sees the same higher cognitive skills or general level knowledge being derived not, or not exclusively, from abstract dialogue but from, or in combination with, various forms of practical experience. The process of acquiring generalised knowledge/skills is not therefore restricted to higher education institutions but potentially realisable in society as a whole and also already takes place in schools and colleges at all levels. It could therefore be integrated with other forms of education and training in and out of employment and was not conceived of as essentially separate from it.

Primary loyalty in this conception was more likely to be expressed to students. Research interests were thought of as no less essential but were given equal weight with teaching rather than accorded primacy over it. Research, especially in the form of

Independent Study, was not however conceived as the exclusive preserve of qualified professionals but as an activity open to students working collectively or individually at all levels from primary school project work upwards and, indeed, a natural and universal human activity.

Like their colleagues above, representatives of this conception assumed that they were themselves good teachers involved in the transfer of knowledge and skills, but the skills and competences whereby students acquired knowledge were regarded as explicit, rather than – as in the rival conception – as implicit to the process of transfer. Teaching was therefore more of a collaborative exercise undertaken with the students' active participation than one in which knowledge was handed down from teacher to students whose role was essentially passive. The nature of the curriculum was also not fixed but problematic, because rapidly changing across subject boundaries and therefore also open to negotiation with students and others.

By contrast, the opposed concept of academic education implied the intensive study of one subject, closely related to research in that subject. It might be therefore described as vocational education for those preparing for work in academic research. Selection for this vocation is seen as through a series of examination hurdles at which the majority fail at every stage. The function of education is thus not so much to teach as to establish the conditions in which the majority of students can fail and the minority sort themselves out for further research, eventually to succeed their examiners as the gatekeepers of 'quality' and 'excellence'.

According to this view, the process of education is therefore not lifelong but culminates in the 'final examination' in which the class of degree is used as an indication of the academic quality of the individual, not as a measure of the level of education attained or of the technical expertise acquired. This individual mental quality is viewed as innate, for students are seen as having distinct levels of ability indicated by the type of final degree they obtain – a mind is either an ordinary mind or 'a first class mind'. This label of a fixed state of election or grace is often given much more importance than the subject studied to obtain it. For in the academic world the class of a candidate's first degree may be quoted for or against him (usually) twenty or thirty years after graduation, although the level of qualification at which graduates find employment as academics is demonstrably a function of the academic labour market at different times. In this sense the degree is also final for the minority who continue their study after it, as it is for the majority for whom it is the last exam they take. However in the employment of the majority of graduates outwith academia, their class of degree may get them through the first screening door of entry to employment but then is rapidly forgotten thereafter. In non-academic employment therefore the class of degree is relatively irrelevant, in comparison with the fact of having a degree at all.

Following from this, it is a curiosity that traditional university regulations forbid retaking exams by those who gain a 2.2 or 3 because at least they got a degree and the attempt to get a better one would be simply too cruel and unusual a punishment to inflict upon candidates who are manifestly not first or upper second material. By contrast, those who failed even to gain a classification may try again as they are unknown quantities. Similarly, candidates may appeal on any grounds except against the academic judgement that has been made of them, as the judgement of a pair (usually) of examiners moderated by an external is deemed infallible.

Unlike in North America, students' examination papers are never returned so that they can learn where they went wrong. There are rarely formal marking schemes and the judgements that are made emanate from the unspoken and unexplained tacit knowledge of the discipline culture into which examiners have been socialised by their undergraduate and postgraduate training in the subject. (See below on exam marking in Fine Art as an example.) In the absence of an explicit and systematic approach anomalies abound. For instance, there are great difficulties in gaining a first but it is virtually impossibile to fail final examinations in a subject like sociology, as compared with one like engineering for example, which permits of very precise answers. Contrariwise, 18 per cent of engineering candidates fail their degree examination but many more gain firsts than do sociology examinees. Examination answers in these latter imprecise areas are marked, as a staff interviewee explained, 'not on the basis of some preconceived view of what the "right" answer is in terms of the outcome of the argument but in terms of the quality of the argument and the verbal fluency with which it is expressed', i.e., largely in terms of levels of literacy, as well as of informational and conceptual content.

Perhaps this accounts in part for the finding that arts and social science students on the whole rarely 'fail' or 'succeed' as spectacularly as science and technology students generally do. It is certainly related to another anomaly, that between men's and women's final degree results. However, the fact that most arts and social science students are female and most science and technology ones are male does not account for the well-established 'clumping' of final exam classifications by gender, with females typically rating seconds against males who outnumber them in firsts and thirds. 'Blind' marking – without knowing the candidate's name – reduces but does not eliminate this outcome.

Those 'soft' academic staff who point to such anomalies and suggest alternatively graded forms of assessment – either just pass or fail with opportunities to retake and/or with portfolios of work graded by average attainment (rather like the modular scheme discussed in the next chapter), are regarded as 'soft' by their academically more 'hard' colleagues. In the course of research at Inner City especially, it was noticeable that staff who made allowances for students, such as replacing an exam paper with a dissertation, or just by extending essay deadlines, were labelled 'soft' by colleagues who urged them to be 'hard' and uphold academic standards and thus their conception of themselves as researchers and scholars, rather than as mere teachers, and of their institution as an academy and not a school.

The various senses of the use of the words 'hard' and 'soft' will be developed further but one can be noted here: 'soft' staff who questioned the rules of the system and the standards by which they and their colleagues had been successful and which provided them with a valued identity, undermined their own position. Like turkeys voting for Christmas, they were regarded by the 'hard' majority at both institutions as perhaps 'soft' in the head, certainly lacking in 'hard' and rigorous logic!

The notion of 'hardness' relates also to the masochistic nature of academic disciplines to which 'hard' cases feel they have subjected themselves, echoing the monastic origins of their craft, and which they sadistically inflict upon others. For in order to gain acceptance in academia, a subject has to be shown to be 'hard', like the 'hard sciences'. This means it is not only 'hard' for students to learn but also for their teachers to be qualified to teach it.

Knowledge is then, following an economic analogy, the more valuable as it is increasingly rare and inaccessible, hard to find and refine – like gold. This involves a contradiction however, as knowledge (as distinct from the mystical experiences or revelations with which it is often confused) by definition only exists so long as it is shared. This accounts for what the anthropologist, Frederick Bailey, investigating the strange academic tribes of North America, described as the academic community's 'fragile sense of superiority ... that curiously nervous elitism, which combines a firm sense of one's own superiority with a conviction that there is no way in which outsiders can be made to acknowledge it'.

There is thus a whole occupational folklore about the trials and rigours of the Ph.D. completion which is coming to be demanded as the standard qualification for higher education teaching – though there are plenty of purely arbitrary exceptions to this, as to other 'rules' of academic selection. It is a 'hardness' which doctorands feel bound to impose upon their postgraduate students. At another level though, this is acknowledged to be something of a ritual. Ph.D. theses are notoriously unreadable and have to be rewritten for publication. The majority of them moulder unread in dusty corners of libraries. Yet postgraduates are expected to plough through them if only to cast their own efforts in the same dry style. Jokes, like that about the Ph.D. supervisor who removed every third page from a thesis because 'It was too long and nobody would notice anyway', reveal the hollowness of the pretence in many cases. It is almost like the mythical Australian tribe whose age-graded generations were inducted each year into greater and more mysterious secrets until, arriving at venerable age, they entered the wisest and most secret society of all where they shared the untellable Great Secret that there were no secrets and all those they had been so awesomely led to believe in were total untruths!

The distinction between 'hard' and 'soft' among HE teachers is the same as that which educational research in schools long ago made between traditional teachers (called 'lion tamers' by one researcher) and 'progressivists' (in relation to what was in the 1960s called progressive primary schooling), 'realists' against 'romantics' in another dichotomising of school teachers. It also corresponds with Bernstein's distinctions – well known in educational sociology – between teachers subscribing to a 'collection' code, with strong classification and framing of the curriculum, as against integrated curricula weakly framed and classified.

Students, incidentally, who do not measure up are not

considered 'soft'. The corresponding terms for students are 'weak' for 'soft' and 'strong' for 'hard' cases. 'Strong candidates' demonstrate their qualities in written examinations in which students are granted marks as a measure of the extent to which their answers approximate to the right answer – that is, the answer preconceived by the examiner. Although students are repeatedly told – especially in the arts and humanities – that there is no right answer, in fact all the different possible acceptable right answers have usually already been worked out for essays and examinations by their markers, however obscure these desired outcomes may remain to students who nevertheless invest great efforts in trying to divine them and make them explicit to themselves.

The range of written communication by students is traditionally very limited, as are oral forms of communication in HE – lecture, seminar, tutorial. Written examination is the most appropriate form to assess the essential knowledge handed down by traditional higher education as this is propositional in form and communicable in writing. (At the extreme, in the 'really hard' mathematics-based sciences, essential knowledge is only expressable as algebraic formulation.) Other sorts of knowledge are not regarded as 'real knowledge'. Nevertheless, the acceptable form for most written presentations – essays, dissertations, theses – is an exercise not primarily in content but in the form of appropriate literary ability and presentation of argument. Indeed, it would be an interesting experiment to present examiners with written work conveying the same information but variously reproduced grammatically and ungrammatically, tidily and untidily, correctly spelt and misspelt, expressed elegantly and haltingly, etc. This would confirm how much marks are given for literary ability as against the actual content.

This emphasis upon form over content is the ultimate in conformity, but it corresponds with the conformity of academic culture which has already been remarked. Particular areas of knowledge, further subdividing existing specialisms, are vigorously defended from encroachment by self-referential journals, specialist conferences and the professorial paternalism which nurtures chosen successors in the style and the culture of the master. 'Citations indices' of the number of (usually repetitive) publications in journals refereed by academic peers function here as a form of intellectual capital, a supposedly 'objective' means of allocating scarce goods. (The spuriousness of these measures is shown by anyone who manages to slip an obvious error past the referees of one of these learned journals – subsequent corrections boosting their citation rating marvellously!)

The processes involved in the supposedly objective procedures of specialist assessment of students were revealed by research at Inner City on the awarding of marks for the fine art end of degree show – the only final award, incidentally, based exclusively upon the product created by students during their course of study and one where (aesthetic) judgement is notoriously subjective. Here the researcher was able to observe that students who followed their tutors too closely in style of art were as unlikely to gain good marks as students who departed completely from the established style of their tutors, as a genuinely original artist presumably would. Aside from proficiency in various techniques which also had to be demonstrated and a certain background knowledge elicited by a paper in art history, highest marks were obtained by those students who were able to follow the style of their tutors, though not so closely as to be judged 'unoriginal'. When it came to the exam board meetings at which marks were allocated, and which the researcher attended, the tutors put forward proportionate numbers of their tutees for the various classifications of degrees. A bargaining process between them then decided how many firsts and upper-seconds would be gained by each tutor's students and how many thirds, the rest going into the uncontentious lower-second category. Once this bargaining process was completed it was confirmed by the external examiner from another higher education institution who came to view the show. The external examiner could however throw the bargaining process open again if he or she disagreed with the provisional marks that had been suggested by the previous board meeting.

When the findings of this research were explained to a biology lecturer at Home Counties, he spontaneously agreed, 'But that's how our exam board works!' Indeed, the system of external examiners upon which so much reliance is placed to maintain comparable standards between higher education institutions, and which is essential to their claim to equal 'quality' across the system and in all subjects, is essentially similar. Another interviewee – at Inner City this time – confided that external examiners rarely raised any objections in any case to the marks which had already been decided in his subject (chemistry) because, 'Most people invite their mates to be external examiners.' Even so, widespread reports indicate this system of external examining is collapsing due to inadequate remuneration for the examiners involved.

The professorial paternalism which manages this system is typically also patriarchal. This is shown by the fact that less than one in twenty of the UK's top academics are women, according to 1993 research by the Association of University Teachers. The unconscious discrimination that produces this imbalance begins with the nurturing of undergraduate students picked out as likely candidates for Ph.D. places by their professorial patrons.

This method of preliminary selection is wide open to abuse, as shown by repeated NUS surveys of their female undergraduate membership, which eventually prodded the university lecturers union (the AUT) into issuing a code of conduct for its members in 1993 on 'consensual relations' with students. (For postgraduates the situation may be worse: a 1993 survey of 500 postgraduate and trainee psychologists – most of them women – revealed nearly half to have had intimate relations with their supervisors that they subsequently regretted. This situation may be peculiar to psychology however!) Male students – as seen – are in any case more likely to gain the first class degrees increasingly necessary to gain funding for postgraduate study. However, one student interviewee at Inner City reported of the cultural studies department, of which he was a minority male member, that it was run by 'a white, middle-class, feminist mafia', so this is possibly not an exclusively masculine trait; just that in most cases, as in society at large, the men got there first.

The Germanic model of subject specialisation, which cross-cuts the collegial system at Home Counties and permeates the managerialist model of the various departments followed at Inner City, can allow the professors who rule their specialist fiefdoms almost feudal powers. However, the former-polytechnics have a culture which tends to recognise the rights of senior people to lead and manage whereas the Oxbridge model of collegial equality tends to subvert this. As one exasperated Home Counties professor reported, 'The consequence is anarchy in the strict sense'. This disorganisation encourages the networks of personal alliances cultivated by academics, whose allegiances – like those of feudal lords – are not to the king, the Vice Chancellor of the institution they work in, but to the lieges to whom they owe fealty or, as a sociologist said, 'to my colleagues primarily'.

Unlike feudal princes however, the mass of traditional

academics more resemble medieval peasants as each tills their own subdivided specialist plot, competing for resources and contributing the minimum to the public good as each acts rationally in their individual circumstances to maximise their own personal prestige in terms of consultancy fees, research grants, publications and so on. Also unlike princes, the professors not only hand on bureaucratic power and patronage, they also safeguard especially the future of their own ideas. As the poet Pope said, 'The mind is enamoured of its own productions' and this personal investment in their own intellectual productions and interpretations perhaps accounts for the peculiarly intense bitterness of many academic disputes and their often personal nature, especially when − as inevitably occurs − the sons revolt against the patronage of their fathers.

The arbitrariness of professorial patronage is however buttressed by elaborate systems for rating their colleagues' work in a supposedly unbiased and 'professional' manner. Needless to say, the system of appointments and promotions, publications and reviews in learned journals and the awarding of research grants is anything but objective. It is necessary to have professorial patronage to get in and get on and professors themselves cultivate their protégés in order to call in at some future date the debts incurred by staff at the commencements of their careers, which accrue in a gearing relation, to a value far in excess of the original small favour done by the professor. Often all this merely encourages deadening conformity, obscurantism and the pursuit of the latest academic fashion, heightened by the absurd system of rating scholarship and research by the outpouring of repetitive and redundant academic publications which it stimulates, which are often, it seems, deliberately obscure.

Ernest Gellner has pointed to 'a setting up of artificial obsolescence and rotation of fashion, characteristic of the consumer industry' in higher education of which the current craze for 'postmodernism' is, he says, symptomatic − 'a highly ephemeral phenomenon, destined for oblivion when the next fad arrives'. As Gellner explained it,

> In the world's most developed countries, something around 50 per cent of the population receives higher education. The colleges and universities which provide it are staffed by people who are assessed in terms not merely of teaching performance but also of intellectual creativity and originality, on the model of an ever-growing natural science, and

of great centres of learning, where scholars find themselves on the very frontiers of knowledge. In routine teaching establishments, and in fields such as the humanities, not only is it not clear that there is any cumulative development, any real 'progress', it is not always altogether clear just what 'research' should or could aim at. So this extensive world of university instruction is run on the model applicable to a few centres of creative excellence, and in genuinely cumulative, expanding natural sciences. There simply must be the appearance of both profundity and originality. It is all intended to resemble scientific growth.

One does not have to share Gellner's faith in the 'few centres of creative excellence' to share his scepticism and to ask as he does, 'But what if there isn't any?' – profundity, originality or scientific growth.

Different concepts of 'the subject'

The origins of the two staff 'hard' and 'soft' conceptions of higher education lay in a fourfold positioning of interviewees, in relation to the subject discipline which they taught as they conceived it and into which they had been socialised by their individual identification with a particular paradigm of their subject specialisation.

1. Staff in new subjects of study, like computer science, where, because the subject was new, there was no fixed body of knowledge and technical expertise to be acquired, but this was normally changing all the time, especially in relation to new technology.

2. Staff in long established subjects of study that were changing primarily in response to external pressures from outside professional bodies, as in the case of physics for instance, but also due to new technology which interrelated previously separate subjects and facilitated information retrieval so that memorisation and other traditional methods of recall and representation were no longer necessary, for example of text book cases in 'black letter' law.

3. Staff in traditionally defined subjects who saw the potentialities presented, especially by the new interrelations made possible by the latest applications of new technology, as well as by modular course structures, to redefine the fixed body of their

subject knowledge into a more dynamic and fluid conception but who were frustrated by existing and constraining discipline boundaries.

4. Staff who defended traditionally defined subjects (though not necessarily long-established ones – sociology being a case in point) whose boundaries, and therefore their own specialised knowledge or expertise, they saw as threatened by: the interconnections made possible by new technology (with which they were themselves often unfamiliar); by modularisation and, still more, by semesterisation (seen as signalling the advent of a teaching-only institution); and by connecting education with employment (seen as 'training'); or by admitting students on the basis of previous experience or other qualifications than conventional 'A' level schooling for higher education (seen as degrading both the institution in the competition for well qualified students and themselves to teachers from their ideal self-conception as researchers or scholars). For them change was of course possible in their subject but was only permissible if gradual, organic and cumulative, building upon the existing canon of set texts, established techniques to be acquired, cases to be learnt, or scientific principles to be followed.

Relation to employment is the crucial variable in this subject typology. The fixed body of knowledge required for 'hard' subjects is only indirectly related, if at all, to its use in employment. The 'harder' a subject is, the more abstract and remote it is from reality, for example traditional philosophy or theoretical physics. Even prestigious subjects which are also vocational because connected to high status employment, like medicine and law, are vulnerable to change from outside – in the professional regulations that they meet accredited by professional bodies. This was the case at both Home Counties and Inner City with law and even physics.

Other subjects defended themselves from such change from outside by assuming a critical and anti-vocational stance. Indeed this was particularly crucial to the self-image of sociology at both institutions and to English at Home Counties. In the latter, one student interviewee recalled,

One of the shocks I had in my second year was when a lecturer in a lecture on Dickens said, 'Well, of course those of you who are going to join the Civil Service…' and I thought, 'Oh my God, is that the sort of thing we're expected to do?', but apart from that work's never mentioned.

The University Careers Service is consequently deliberately eschewed by many students, at least, in the words of the Head of the Service at Home Counties, 'Until the last minute when it's too late'; especially as,

> If they've got anything less than a 2.1 – unless with a 2.2 they can really impress an employer with all their extra-curricular activities, then they might just scrape through – but if they've got a third or a pass, they might as well forget it, not come to the Careers Service at all and just look in the paper or visit the job centre, make a plan to resurrect their career by stealth.

Separating instead of integrating careers education into the curriculum sustained, he thought, 'fantasy choices' in students as a way of putting off any real decision, 'working in the media' being amongst the most popular. When these 'fantasy choices' eventually came up against reality and students failed to find employment, then

> they can blame the system – say it's too cut-throat – and retreat grace-fully to teaching, or put off decision a bit longer by travelling around the world.

(Strangely, despite its relatively advantageous position in the hierarchy of HEIs, Home Counties' destination list of graduate first employment showed a higher percentage unemployed than Inner City's. This was because the university was not in the top fifteen or so prestigious institutions which, depending on subject mix, are closely targeted by the top graduate employing organisations. Many of its graduates, without any previous work experience, and reluctant to lower their sights from the type of jobs they had been led to expect, were therefore left high and dry. By contrast, Inner City graduates were more prepared to accept 'grotty' jobs if only temporarily and, having got in, often on the basis of previous experience, sometimes got on. Also, many Asian students returned to working with their families if they did not immediately find the posts for which their graduate studies qualified them.)

This academic distance from any vocational involvement is deliberate. Especially English and sociology, but other arts and humanities also, have set themselves as subjects in opposition to the dominant 'Benthamite utilitarianism' of the age, as the twentieth century's greatest English literary critic, F.R. Leavis, described what many sociologists would see themselves exposing as the consequences of untrammelled free-market capitalism. This is of course a valuable assertion of critical independence which should be preserved, but it must be recognised that it is also a counter in the academic power game by which a group of professional teachers tries to preserve its professional self-interest and relatively privileged position. The assertion is the more desperate in 'non-vocational subjects', as they see themselves and as they are seen by others. For in the new order which is threatened, they would be reduced to teaching-only status; they have already for a long time been predominantly feminine subjects, with a majority of female students if not staff – another mark of low status in the academic hierarchy.

Representatives of all the four positions above in relation to employment and to their self-conception of their subject of study could be found at both institutions amongst all subjects. Indeed, they are clearest illustrated by two fine art lecturers at Inner City. For one of these, fine art education was studio-based or it was nothing. For the other, 'Education is part of a process in constant change not something fixed.' Education could therefore potentially take place anywhere, and this lecturer spoke of 'letting go' and 'going with the flow', 'not being afraid of change'.

Similarly a Home Counties lecturer in computer science stated,

> I know it sounds like a cliché but we are now working in a culture of change where we've taken on board the notion that change is fun and stimulating rather than being terrifying and destructive.

In this new and developing subject area, a traditional discipline body of knowledge was not established, but information and techniques were necessarily (and constantly) changing. So that

> There's no notion that the primary purpose of the university is to turn out academics. That notion is totally outmoded nowadays if only because of the numbers involved. Degrees have to cater for people who are going to go into a wide range of occupations.

The skills involved therefore were already explicit, so that for example,

> We've had communication skills integrated into what computer science students are doing anyway for a number of years. We have looked at what it involves to work with others, write reports, make presentations,

etc., and built those into the course. The area is changing the whole time so the idea that you could teach the same course for ten years is not how we work at all. It's not just 'the bloke' doing one chapter per week in 'the course of the book'.

Indeed, such a prospect of teaching was regarded by this interviewee as 'horrific'.

There is increasing emphasis in the computing lab on working in groups – self-teaching and peer tutoring with staff-run clinics. Just because the faculty is so large, it has to be divided up into working groups. Plus with the modularisation of courses, we're divided up into course teams and you've got to meet regularly to deliver the course effectively. But we're also in a position where nobody is ever by and large giving a course by themselves.

The set-text, 'course of the book' method of learning that a number of student interviewees at Home Counties also remarked upon was rejected by this staff member,

because we are moving away from a situation where all our students do all our courses. We don't have the idea that if you have more students you put on more courses.

This was compared with other (traditional) subjects where,

The idea is that there is this vast body of knowledge that everybody has to be dragged through kicking and screaming, so you would tend just to push more into the lectures.

Instead,

If students want to do weird and wonderful combinations, let them get on and do it, but most students don't do things like that. If a student wants to do a mixture of things and it's on the timetable – not that we should bust a gut to get every possible combination on the timetable – then that's fair enough. The students can just fight their way through, provided you're doing enough of each subject to get the progression necessary – you can't just dot about all over the place – because you can't do a second year course that involves writing programmes if you didn't do the first year course that taught you the basic programming techniques, for instance.

As a result, this interviewee had no worries about what others opposed to her 'soft' view referred to disparagingly as a 'cafeteria system' of 'pick'n'mix' modules.

By contrast, the majority of Home Counties interviewees and a minority of Inner City ones felt that to change traditional methods was to 'surrender to the logic of the market', 'subordinate education for its own sake to training for employment', or even 'to drown in the post-modern flux'. For them, because students were constituted as a market, to accede to student demand would inevitably weaken the academic content of courses because students would choose 'soft' options or merely what was vocationally prescribed. Instead, they had to be 'dragged kicking and screaming', as the 'soft' computer scientist put it above, through 'the great body of knowledge' that made up the curriculum, and were not in a position to decide to do otherwise since, due to the cumulative nature of courses, they would not see the point of the exercise until they had completed it.

It was therefore impossible to be more explicit about course content and higher education was already in any case delivering the so-called 'personal and transferable skills' demanded by employers and government, and written examinations were a suitable way to assess them. The Home Counties' option system was also seen by these 'hard' interviewees there as already providing sufficient student choice. Further modularisation was likely only to result in dismantling carefully constructed and intellectually cumulative courses. More students, especially at Home Counties, inevitably meant a worsening of quality and therefore the gold standard of 'A' level entry should be maintained for standard entry students well prepared by their previous schooling, with the exception only of a minority of mature students or 'non-standard' entrants with qualifications other than 'A' level for whom occasional, generous allowances could exceptionally be made. These interviewees could see only problems and not opportunities in any other approach.

At the same time, individuals holding such 'hard' conceptions often contradicted themselves by complaining about their students. At Home Counties students were regarded by many staff as 'arrogant' and unthinkingly conventional, while at Inner City students were sometimes the butt of jokes about their 'inability to do joined-up thinking', and etc. At Home Counties seminar leaders in the humanities and social sciences often hoped that their seminar groups would be enlivened by the presence of a mature student or two, who on the basis of their experience 'have so much more to say than the young kids'. Yet the suggestion that the university change its entry requirements to admit more such unconventionally qualified (i.e., non-'A' level) students was rejected

by most staff there who insisted upon the importance of 'maintaining high entry standards'.

The extra work that this might entail, giving students who did
not possess them as a result of their previous schooling and upbringing the skills to deal with an unchanged academic curriculum, was resented by 'hard' academics as detracting from the
research and scholarship they regarded as their primary and
essential interest. This was the practical source of their opposition
to expansion in student numbers, even though as liberal-minded
people – which most of them were (to an extent anyway) – they
would in theory be in favour of widening access to higher education beyond an elite (see further below). Certainly humanities and
social science staff at Home Counties talked a great deal about
their research interests, even if they did not perhaps themselves
do quite as much research as all this talk about it indicated.

It can be added here that the belief that research is part of the
core meaning of higher education is essentially ideological. Cardinal Newman, who has been described as 'the household god of
the liberal university', in his canonical 'The Idea of a University',
for instance, believed that research should be undertaken in institutions other than universities. So it can be said that research is
not an essential part of the process of higher education as such
and that course design is better led by educational and not research objectives. Indeed, especially at postgraduate level where
students are often taken on to assist in large scale research projects,
this often pushes them into following the research director's
priorities and not their own. However, any questioning of the
central dogma of the unity of teaching and research was regarded
as playing into the government's hands. (Instead, we will argue
further that, as an essential part of their education, all students –
as well as all staff – should be involved in some sort of research,
discovery or creation.)

Again, Home Counties staff would often agree, for instance,
that the seminar system did not manifestly work as it was intended
to in many cases, or as it had worked in some mythically receding
past of lower numbers. Since the seminar system was also regarded
as the distinguishing feature of the quality higher education to
which the University aspired, this was quite an admission. Yet
they rejected any proposal to change either seminars or the examinations which they also readily agreed were an inadequate form
of assessment. Over the years, they would assure the interviewer,

every possible alternative to them had been tried, and written examinations were the best of a bad bunch, tempered perhaps with other methods to up to no more than 20 per cent of the marks.

Written exams therefore had to be persisted with, even though they too were becoming impossible to mark under the weight of numbers. In fact, this was an argument for restricting numbers – rather than for changing assessment procedures. Consequently the 'hard' majority of academics adhering to unchanging methods in face of changing circumstances were described by a member of the 'soft' minority as 'perpetual seekers after excuses' not to change, rather than as the seekers after knowledge they were supposed to be. Thus it has been well said that, 'The worst vice of higher education is its complacency.'

To take an example, a Home Counties sociologist considered,

> I think in what I do there is quite a lot of attention to what might be called 'skills'.

He thought of the skills of academic education as subject-centred:

> The skills are being able to acquire knowledge in your given subject area – search catalogues, read around a subject not just what's on the reading list, being able to read a book not necessarily from cover to cover but to get maximum return in minimum time, writing, cramming for exams – which is an overrated skill but still quite useful because at other points in your life you're going to have to cram knowledge for other purposes, and the skills of personal presentation in seminars.

In addition, it might sometimes be necessary, as he put it,

> to give first aid to students who require help in certain areas but I'm not going to spend my time in doing what should have been done at secondary level.

(This despite the University having admitted the student!) Similarly with so-called 'personal transferable skills', including the use of new technology,

> I don't see why that should be part of my duties. It's not often that I've said to a student, 'Look this is impossible to read, why don't you learn how to do word processing?' but I would hope that would encourage [*sic*!] them in that particular aspect of skills acquisition.

By contrast, Inner City students were told from the first to hand in word-processed scripts as this facilitated marking and correction, ideally in the form of draft and then final versions incorporating the workshop facilitator's and sometimes other students' comments if there was time for this.

As a professor of modern languages, representative of the predominant 'hard' conception at Home Counties, put it,

> Every lecturer knows that the biggest challenge for students coming up to university is to organise themselves and their time after coming out of what tends to have been a rather structured organisation to a situation where there is very little structure at all. They learn to manage budgets by living away from home, and if you're thinking about how to generate independent, competent people who can stand on their own two feet then the British system is an extraordinarily efficient way of doing it.

(This, of course, assumed a standard age of student entrant.) She continued,

> I've always felt most strongly that university is about skills training and I think that we have tended not to have been up-front enough about it. The ability to write a well-structured, well-argued essay for instance is an extraordinarily useful skill which can then be applied to an enormous number of other situations and if our seminars are about anything they are about helping students to think clearly. This is an extraordinarily useful skill that is applicable in almost any walk of life.

Everything necessary was therefore already being done and there was no need to change it. It was not perfect but other approaches had been tried in the past and invariably did not work so well. For all its imperfections this was therefore the best of all possible worlds.

Languages were conceived differently by a junior lecturer in the same department, as

> not limited to the literature of the country but involving so many other things – the geography and history, the culture of the country – if we don't change then we stagnate, especially in the language which changes every day.

This view contrasted with that of many of her colleagues who thought of their subject in terms of a canon of literary texts making up the national literature of the language that was only gradually being added to, if at all, and in the case of classical Greek and Latin was by definition complete. With this different conception of the subject, skills were conceived differently:

> Skill teaching in my view is achieving the objectives through methods which not only involve theoretical explanation and exposition of ideas but also through practical and innovative tasks and these are the ones that I'm testing through the development and extension of such ideas by the learner. Therefore I think that skills enhance learning. If they can see the practical application of certain learning I believe that students give more effort. This is definitely a new method of learning. It also relates more directly to their future employment.

Physics is a subject which faces changes to its curriculum, primarily in response to the pressure of external professional bodies. As the staff member interviewed at HCU explained,

> Physics used to be a body of theoretical knowledge but it became overloaded... and we're wondering are we teaching them the right things.

Physicists were therefore introducing an explicit skills emphasis to their curriculum and this was not seen as opposed to traditional academic values, even if it was vocationally related because,

> It can [also] broaden the base which students look at in terms of employment. [But] this is traditional as well because the Institute of Physics is always saying how physics is not a vocational degree.

> Employers are always complaining about scientists in industry whom they see as rather naive, too theoretical; they don't know how to apply things and they are bad communicators. They have in a sense to learn new skills of a technological kind but they need the mathematical ability to adapt to that. I think physicists have problems adapting because they've been taught everything in a rather general way. They have to go through a sort of intermediate training to adapt and be flexible.

Of all the subjects at Home Counties, law had adopted the most thorough-going revision of teaching in the incorporation of skills, partly as with physics at the prompting of external professional bodies, but partly in line with long-held values among some of the teachers. In this revision, a law lecturer revealed,

> Skill teaching in my view is achieving the objectives through methods which not only involve theoretical explanation and exposition of ideas but also through practical and innovative tasks, and these are the ones that I'm testing through the development and extension of such ideas by the learner. That is to say that I think that... if students can see its practical application, learning is enhanced by skills.

The cultural change involved in this approach was also stressed by a Home Counties historian running a new course involving work on nearby archaeological sites:

> If you're on this course you're going to have to get up in the morning, which you know for most students is not a high thing on their agenda. You must get up, you must appear and you must keep it up, which you know doesn't appeal to most students.

As for himself, he no longer felt 'bored' by his students, as he had previously:

> It's the most exciting thing I have done for years – which is probably a sad reflection on my life actually!

The course contrasted with the traditional approach because

> At the end of the day the students had more to take away than just a body of knowledge, than just some 'information'. The traditional approach is related to a body of knowledge, especially in history – the emphasis is on amassing this body of knowledge and then regurgitating it in intelligent form. In English it's not so much a body of knowledge as training people how to read a body of literature and getting the most out of it. [But] history should help you not only to amass the body of knowledge but to communicate the analysis and drive the thing home.
>
> So I hope that they will think that 'Going to old Smith's lectures taught me how to suss things out on my feet'. So I don't see myself teaching people to become historians because most of them won't. Sadly this is the approach of a number of my colleagues. They wouldn't actually formulate it to you in an interview like this but a lot of their thinking suggests that that's what they do think and sometimes they actually say it. Sometimes at board meetings people say we must gear the syllabus so that students can become history masters and mistresses but this is mistaken because that is not what most of them do. They go into Marks and Spencer and the Civil Service and marketing and all sorts of things.

Similarly,

> I personally have no fears or worries about modularisation because I've taught in the American system. What it comes down to is teaching one course per term and I'm a great believer in a quick burst, a great in-put and then giving them a rest and letting them go on to something else. This is backed up by psychologists and so on who have written endless boring papers and studied lectures in progress which show that the lecturer's input in the first quarter of an hour has a mega-impact on them – they're taking notes and so on; they're alive

– then the next ten minutes there's an exponential drop in this thing and after half an hour it's almost brain-death. That is the American view and it's in contradiction to the traditional view, building it all up with very large cement blocks weighing you down. In the semester view you build it up with lots of little blocks. But you need motivated students. If they're too laid-back it doesn't work. It's all over before it begins.

The promised land must always be in sight for students. They have to know where they're going and a good teacher should say 'Now this is what we hope to achieve and this is how we're going to achieve it and the promised land is when we have achieved it and the promised land is X, Y and Z.' Now on short courses the promised land is easier to envisage.

This approach and the explicitness that it involved was antithetical to the opposed 'hard' majority of academic interviewees. For them the much disputed term 'quality' was essentially inexplicable because it was related to open rather than closed outcomes. 'Like defining love,' as a professor of English literature said with reference to a poem by W.H.Auden,

> Everybody knows what it is and what it is isn't but such is the nature of the beast that you can't give a pithy definition. I take it that a quality course involves a coherent body of work such that one bit of it would shed light on another bit of it, so you're not doing units but it's cumulative in its effect and it adds up to more than the sum of its parts. The things that are being studied are worthwhile in any one of a number of possible ways. The teacher is committed, open-minded and knowledgeable and the students develop as they go along, improve their capacity to set down ideas clearly as they go along. You can't have a general rubric.

Short modular courses with explicable outcomes such as those advocated by the history professor were characteristically seen by this interviewee as 'a cafeteria' or 'pick'n'mix'. The culinary comparison was, however, accepted by the history professor above who argued,

> There's no reason why we can't channel them in the cafeteria to take decent food. You'd probably need a core because I would hold onto one traditional element and that is, you know, although we're training them ultimately to think for themselves I'm also a great believer in, for their own self-respect, they need to come out saying 'Well, I know something about history, or social psychology or biology or whatever it is'. So I'm all for mixing in side dishes on the fringes but there would

need to be a main course which is their main course. It would have to be staff led but giving them sufficient choice that they could feel they were constructing their own degree within the parameters that we give them. Especially for the professional degrees, you just must have that core of specified material. But I think maybe we're moving in the American direction where there's a lot of choice at first degree level but then when it comes to the second degree there's no messing, it's law or whatever as it ever was.

The new type of degree course

As explained by a principal lecturer in engineering at Inner City University the new type of degree course entailed 'students taking responsibility for their own learning'.

This means designing their own course from a portfolio of options which will be rather a large number of unit options – 60 or 70 of them. Students will have to take a common first year and choose a common core. That core could be industrial studies, or computer aided design. Now having chosen the core they will have to choose units from designated core units and design their degree around that core. This might seem very limiting but it means there are something like 150,000 possible degree pathways.

Now what you've got to do is justify your choice and as you progress you will have to build on what you have already done in the degree. It will have to be developmental in terms of content not just of transferable skills. And then monitoring their progress on the course, students will have to carry with them their log book or diary of achievement. They will have to reflect on their own learning. We will monitor it as well of course.

When students choose their course they will probably chose it from topics, for instance on statistical quality control, and they will be able to use this computer package to get the course content specified. They will also be able to ask the question in terms of what skills they want to develop – of information retrieval, or presentation skills, or mathematical or computing skills. Where's the best set of modules to develop these skills from? Critical path analysis, linear programming for optimising constituents, fish bone diagrams – all the little techniques of this type that go into management courses and will be useful in other jobs, not only for managing this particular factory.

Group work for instance, what does that mean in the context of this module? It means doing experiments in the laboratory where you've got to book your own time and sort out how you're going to do your experiment with the other people involved. Or it could be case study where group work means discussing collectively with other students the problems of this company. So we can give chapter and verse what group work means in this particular module, which will be different in different modules, making explicit what is in the course content in terms that make sense to the student not how we define it.

What we're trying to do is give students a choice of modules but give them that choice from a sensible position, not just give them a syllabus because you probably don't know what it means, as the students don't know. I mean, it can have aims and objectives but these are usually written for other members of staff and especially when you list the content, that probably only has meaning to someone who's an expert in the subject anyway and is totally meaningless to the intelligent layperson, which is what the student is when they're starting off.

So if you want to learn how to make presentations, what making presentations in this subject means is this: 'dah, dah, dah'. If you want to learn statistical skills in this subject, this is how we use statistics. This is very different from how we would have thought of it before and this is where the counselling role comes in, to explain what the real agenda is. It makes the staff think more explicitly about what they're doing, because of course we've always done experiments, we've always used statistics and so on, but it means thinking in a slightly different way to make the approach consistent across the board. It's what the subject area demands and what our resources allow us to deliver.

So what we are doing when we write the modules that we've got on offer in addition to content and one or two other things that are useful, such as the assessment procedures and the staff involved, is to list the transferable skills being developed in these modules, if any. So we can design their course both from content and from the skills developed in it. Then all the students have to do is come to the tutor with a provisionally validated proposal and then we'll tell them whether they can do it. Whether there are ten people on this module or not and if there aren't they can't do it. That could also be written into the programme but in practice they'll work it out together, collectively by negotiation.

Let me give you an example in terms of experiments: you can say to students next week turn up to the lab and the 12 of them will divide into three groups of four and you can stay around for three or four hours while they each perform the experiments in their groups, then hopefully they write it up. But that's very unsatisfactory because you have very little time with each student and the lab is very crowded while for the rest of the week it's empty. So you can easily give the student a handout at the beginning of the course which says these are the labs you have to do, now you can either do them on your own or with other people and you can fit them in when you want but you'll have to go and book the lab with the technician concerned and there'll be a member of staff there to show you how to use any equipment and answer any specific questions.

Students reading the handout will see the books that they need to refer to and presumably, if the lectures are related to the lab work, they'll attend regularly, be a bit more diligent, and sort it out with friends – you know, 'What does this mean?' – not reading the handout as you do the experiment but have sorted it out before hand and anything that isn't clear in the explanation.

This means that there'll be a steady-state population in the laboratory and they'll look very different with text books available in the laboratory and it should be a happier working environment and a member of staff doesn't have to be there all the time, although a technician has to be there and staff will be available.

Now when we're doing that we have to act as the facilitator of the students' learning rather than the fount of their knowledge. In fact, we've got to think in terms of teaching to plan and time management and technicians have to become supervisors while staff are freed to do what they want, pursue their own research and so on. It should be better and it should be more fun as well.

Although modules will fragment their learning they will also improve their choice. You have to cut the content actually because we won't have as much time as we traditionally had. To speed things up, again making students more responsible, we're teaching them to a text book on the American model and there'll be roughly one text book per module. That'll mean us changing what we teach to what's in the book and that is a poor thing that happens in this scheme compared with previously when there were handouts and lectures which were distillations of several textbooks. It depends then on the quality of the textbook but nothing ever quite fits unless you write it yourself, which is the incentive for writing books [but led in turn, as seen, to 'the course of the book' syndrome].

Assessment will be the same – nine exams and nine course work marks in each module, a little formula for passing the module in relation to the content. In computing for instance, it will be 100 per cent course work but in maths we've got to check they really can do it, so it'll be 60 per cent exam.

We're fairly pragmatic in engineering without debating the philosophy of it too much and this will also be a way of attracting students because, let's face it – cards on the table –, if you've got lots of students who want to come on your courses you haven't got much incentive for changing them, have you? The way we got the degree started was we went round to employers and asked them if they would like people with these skills and put it to them that if you will sponsor them – give them a few bob to buy books and give them the time off – then I think you will have a more efficient production environment and not surprisingly they said yes. We've also become quite competent at assessing prior experiential employment for people who want to do the degree part-time. In fact, I think that is now where the main market will be. Since the recession it's been increasingly difficult to get students sponsored so we changed back towards studentships for professional engineers and now we are doing both. With the upgrading of the polytechnic to university we're in a much better position to start marketing the department.

Such a course design seems radical in comparison with the traditional academic degrees at Home Counties where there was little incentive to change in most arts and social science subjects, which were heavily oversubscribed, sometimes reportedly by as many as ten applicants to a place. But the process of course reconstruction had been taken even further by a lecturer in business studies at Inner City. As he described it this was:

A part-time course in which there are no lectures. All the lectures are videotaped so if the students want to look at a video they can do it. It helps me as a teacher because it frees my time. I have more time to apply the same method to the full-time course. It helps them as part-timers. Secondly, they can pick their own course of options. Because last year – before we changed it – I was giving a lecture on manufacturing accounting and at the end of the lecture I turned to them and asked how many of them worked in manufacturing industry and not one of them did, so what was the relevance of what I was teaching them?

They can also pick their own assessment methods. They have to sign a learning contract. They have to include one numerical problem solving exercise and one written descriptive one but the rest is up to them. They have real difficulties deciding because it's not all structured for them. There's no set questions; it's just, 'Advise John'.

Why do you have to wait till the end of the year before you have to regurgitate everything up? Being brought up in the American system I still can't understand that. Students can progress as they please. Why wait a whole year if they can do it straight away? Why do we hold them back that way? If they can run let them run. So I give them a choice when they can take their assessment. Every individual should be allowed to work at his or her own pace. Putting people through this forced speed and design, it's like this age thing in Britain some jobs have age limits on them. Why? If a 50 year old can do the job, hire the 50 year old. So the idea that people are constrained by things they cannot control – their age, their looks, their gender, the colour of their skin, it's irrelevant. Give them a chance to be everything they want to be. If they can take a degree in one year, let them do it. That's not to lower standards; standards stay the same. Quality need not be compromised. Indeed, it mustn't be. That's why I'm against attendance. Attendance only guarantees physical presence. I want mental presence.

Students are ultimately my judge because they are my customers. They are the MacDonald's generation. They want quick, attractive, to the point things; they don't have time to get into these long debates about life. Right or wrong I don't tell. My job is to make them the best students I can. If I get good students that makes my job easier but if they are not so good it doesn't change my job. My tactics will change. Strategies I may apply to the part-time mature students will be different to those I apply with younger students.

I'm not a pure academic, who sounds to me like someone who has given up on the real world. My viewpoint is somewhat tainted by teaching business and finance which I don't consider a subject in the same sense as philosophy or literature. It's a practical skill and, yes, it has some theoretical base in it but people coming here to read business and accountancy are not coming here for some educational purpose – to become more civilised – but to get a good job.

If you take away the incentive of a good job I would like to know how many people will come to the Business School! For instance, we don't teach the theory of double-entry accounting, we just teach how it is done. We don't say this author said this and this author said this, now you make your mind up. No, we say this is the way it is done. It's just skill. I think you will find the same in law. I'm not talking about all business education but a chartered accountant, what is it? Not a theoretician or a philosopher, just someone who does your books.

The basic skills involved are communications, decision making – can you think on your feet? Not just can you do quadratic equations. I'm trying to satisfy employers that we are concentrating on these basic skills, not just teaching them theory. There are ethical issues involved as well of course, for instance in auditing. In the end what I want of a student is someone who, given an unstructured, undefined situation, makes sense out of it and I think having an accounting background helps but it's only a tool.

I think there are two things involved. One is whether we can change our students' attitudes and, two, whether we can change employers' attitudes. I'm trying to make a fundamental thought process change in the students and one of the projects I'm requesting this year takes a cradle to the grave approach from the day the student comes into the university until he or she leaves it, everything has to be oriented towards getting a job – a three or four year marathon, not just leaving it to the final year and 'Oh, I'll send out my CV and do the milk round' because I don't think that will do any more. Those days are long gone now. It's much more competitive.

I was talking to my students in the final year and I said, 'When you get a job' and they said, 'What job? We're not going to get a job'. So it's how to motivate them because they think it's the end of the line for them. You take away the dreams of a 22 year old and he's gone forever. If young people don't dream who can have dreams? But things are very bad for them out there. It's not just that they are not going to get a job but that they are not going to get the job they want. So it's not just jobs, it's expectations.

A skills approach will broaden their horizons because skills are applicable in any field. The employer will say, 'Yes, you have a qualification in accounting and finance but what else can you do for me?' Confidence – that's what it is all about because we all know people who have bluffed their way through life.

This interviewee, as representative of the most logical extreme of the 'soft', student- and skills-centred approach, would certainly confirm the worst fears of those 'hard core' academics who saw modular curricula as 'cafeteria' serving up fast and unsubstantial fare to an uncritical MacDonald's generation and who saw in the emphasis upon 'skills' only superficial exercises in self-presentation – 'bluffing', as he put it. Certainly his views appear self-contradictory in his dismissal of any knowledge beyond the occupationally relevant and yet his acknowledgement that 'personal and transferable' skills were also important if only to increase students' confidence in the 'cradle to the grave' vocationalism that he advocated. Similarly, he hoped to instill such confidence so as not to take away the students' dreams and to give a vocational emphasis to all courses despite the lack of occupational opportunities that he recognised.

Both of these modular approaches, it was evident, from their descriptions by the two members of staff, involved a reduction in both vocational/professional competence and academic subject specific information, as well as (possibly) in general level, 'cognitive' knowledge/skill. Indeed, the first interviewee admitted that there had been a reduction in content on the course. This was not an inevitable consequence of modularisation, but had been a change coincident with the change over from the traditional B.Eng. to the new modularised B.Sc. This now catered for students who previously had been regarded as at technician (Higher National

Diploma) level and who exercised 'supervisory' rather than 'professional' roles in engineering employment. It was a response to a drop in demand for the former B.Eng. graduates. (Not that what was formally technician level work in engineering had remained unchanged; it now demanded additional 'transferable skills' which employees would have to exercise flexibly in this employment as in others and these were attested by and justified the degree qualification of the new course.)

However, not only the informational content of subject specific academic knowledge as well as vocationally relevant techniques and competences may have been lost. There is evidence in the interviews to suggest that general level knowledge of reasoning and scientific or logical thinking had also been reduced. This is particularly so in the second, business studies degree course which did not aspire to 'civilise' its students or turn them into 'philosophers' or 'theoreticians'. Here general level knowledge/skill, applicable to more than vocationally specific situations even if previously developed within the boundaries of a narrowly traditional discipline, had been reduced to techniques and competences specified in advance. These were applicable only or mainly in employment, even if not merely in one particular type of work but applied 'flexibly' across related fields.

Like other advocates of modular systems of learning in different and not necessarily directly vocational courses of study, these interviewees would presumably hope for the development of higher level cognitive skills, or of what we have called generalised knowledge, through student application to the various modules they studied to discover common rules about rules and similar means of mentally dealing with different types of information. At least the modules that they referred to were all within discrete subject areas, even if the second interviewee did not regard his vocational specialism as the equivalent of other more academic disciplines. The staff and their students did not therefore face the problems of integrating modular programmes of study in which students migrate across subject boundaries. These will be examined in the next chapter to question whether reduction in information and knowledge is an inevitable result of modularisation.

We then go on in the last chapter to ask whether, even on the most vocationally specific courses, it would not be possible to combine general with vocational knowledge. This would require a rational pedagogy that began by examining the students' situation in education and in society, building up from the particular to the general and facilitating transfer between them via independent study. First however, we look at the shared situation of higher education staff that might provide the basis for such a common pedagogical response to their contrasted situations in the market hierarchy of institutions.

Shared problems, divided responses

Courses like those described above would be anathema to the hard men (mostly) of Home Counties and those sharing their views at Inner City, typically the sociologists, who could justify a traditional and elitist pedagogic conception of their subject with ultra-left political opinions by reference to quotations from Gramsci (though not the same quotations as we used in chapter one!). Yet while holding such opposed views, all staff also voiced common concerns. At both universities they felt pressurised by the external forces of the government and the market, by management interference and by lack of resources. The result, especially for women, was that, as an Inner City lecturer reported

> Trying to do anything apart from work, trying to get the children to the dentist, for instance – it's a Herculean task.

So that even a woman Professor at Home Counties could report,

> My colleagues' morale is rock bottom and there are certainly moments when I think of getting out. The whole time one is struggling against not having enough money. It's as simple as that.

There was also a common perception that, as an Inner City fine art lecturer put it,

> The most difficult problem for teachers at BA level now is the diversity of quality that's coming in. I mean, in the first year you've got some students who are really excellent and you've got some who, although they've got potential, can hardly cobble a sentence together. [So that] You can't take it for granted that if you mention Plato, for instance, they'll know who you're talking about.

Even at Home Counties one law lecturer reported,

> This year for the first time in lectures I've found myself pausing sometimes, wondering will they understand.

In addition, he added,

There is a twist to the problem of overloading in that the extra students we're getting take up more time.

Many staff at both universities had rationed their contact time (again contributing to the universal student impression that staff were only interested in their research, while staff felt they were 'lecturing to a sea of heads' and 'dealing with numbers not people'). Indeed, at Inner City one tutor had to explain to a tearful student that she could not see her at weekends 'because I'm not her parent, but that's what she needed'.

As well as this particular problem that larger numbers brought to academic professionals, another Home Counties lecturer claimed to detect a general change in students entering university from school. He related this to 'changes in the schools, even in the primary schools.' As a result of the Technical and Vocational Education Initiative (the school and further education equivalent of the Higher Education Initiative), as well as from changes in the GCSE exams if not 'A' levels,

> They seem to be more open minded but the foundation that they're working from seems to be getting a little bit weaker. Perhaps it's tipping just a bit too far, too superficial, too conceptual without the basis for it. So I think that's the difference – students are becoming more enquiring but perhaps they lack the ammunition they need to deal with it.

Others attributed such general changes to the ubiquitous influence of the aural and visual media, so that a professor of English could say that,

> Students no longer live in a literary culture. They have to learn to read even Victorian novels – let alone Chaucer and Shakespeare – as the products of a foreign culture.

Whatever the cause, the common demand at both institutions was for an increase in resources. Both places were felt to be at a crisis point beyond which

> I don't think you can go on increasing numbers and not have more staff or resources. It will go down beyond this point (Inner City fine art lecturer).

> More students without more resources means worse education. That's all there is to it (Home Counties law lecturer).

This did not mean, as another interviewee stated, that

more necessarily means worse but if you are going to deal with more students you've got to do things differently in terms of resources and access to open learning and so on, all of which could actually lead to an increase in quality. But staff need time to make it work and you just don't have time to prepare for these numbers, to structure these classes of 40 and more. You can manage it. I mean, they've been managing classes of 30 in schools for years but it takes time and organisation which we're just not going to get. So there will be a decline in quality (Inner City business studies lecturer).

He continued,

It requires an awful lot of structuring to enable a mass number of students to reach those outcomes. So I would look for quality in the amount of resourcing and planning given to HE and that isn't happening. Because we are sort of hit we just lurch from pillar to post really, from one crisis to another and we just don't have sufficient planning and time to deal with it. It's not that we couldn't do it but it all comes down to resourcing. I think it needs some pump-priming at least to make the change over, not by trying to make savings as you go along and increase the pressure from year to year. That's a recipe for muddling through. I'm pessimistic because I don't think we have got the resources to respond as we should do and the students are being short-changed by not being able to speak to members of staff when they want to and not being able to get books in the library when they want to and the general lack of planning and structure. They complain all the time about things, particularly the library – not being able to get a quiet place to sit down and do their work. They can't get the books so we have to give them handouts.

Impending modularisation at Home Counties and semester-isation at Inner City were anticipated with foreboding by nearly all staff interviewed:

It's going to be chaos because of the speed and the resources we have been given to do it in (Inner City new technology lecturer).

As a result, nearly all interviewees were extremely pessimistic about likely future developments. For example,

What I think will happen? There will be more numbers without increase in resources. The staff student ratio will be squeezed so they won't get such a good education and the reliance upon non-staff directed methods of learning will go past the point at which those techniques are useful and go into the area where they represent a deterioration of the standard of education given (Home Counties biology lecturer).

That there were grounds for these complaints was clearly shown by a survey for the Association of University Teachers undertaken at Home Counties at the same time as our interviews there were conducted. This showed that out of 92 replies from teaching and research staff, a response rate of 26 per cent, all reported an increase in their teaching load and in the size of typical seminar groups. Teaching had risen by 20 per cent to just over 10 hours per week and seminar sizes to 12.3 on average. These changes were more or less uniform across faculties, although humanities staff reported the highest teaching hours (11.8, compared with 8.2 elsewhere in the University). This contrasted with a rule of thumb measure at Inner City of 15 hours per week teaching and seminar groups of 20. However, these figures had remained standard there for some time.

Similarly, Home Counties respondents to the survey reported a 31 per cent decrease in the proportion of time they spent doing research, most staff giving about one day a week to these activities compared with nearly two days five years previously. This compared with Inner City, starting from a low research base in which emerging research was held by pockets of expertise where it was under threat from rising student numbers, while other areas where there had been no research previously were now finding room for it for the first time.

As to administrative duties, which were also a common cause of complaint among staff interviewees, the Home Counties AUT survey reported a 42 per cent increase in administrative time to over a third of the working week. Scientists reported more time spent on administration than other staff. Numbers of tutees for whom respondents were responsible had also risen over the five year period to nearly 15. This compared with Inner City which officially operated at a 16:1 student:staff ratio.

The responses to these shared circumstances varied by the 'hard' or 'soft' orientation of self to subject that has been outlined. Staff in both camps could agree that more resources were needed both to continue traditional approaches with larger numbers of students and to develop new approaches which were nearly always more staff intensive, at least initially. However, they soon diverged when it came to which direction and conception of education should be followed in future. For instance,

> What I think ought to happen is that we ought to try to develop ourselves some understanding of what a proper education ought to entail

and as far as I can see the traditional form of education has some very desirable aspects to it. What I would like to see as a goal is that everybody in the country has the opportunity to undertake a full course of education up to and including degree level in which the object of the exercise is to develop their knowledge and critical faculties on their own account, that is to say, in and for itself not linked to employment as a main aim. I don't accept that everybody can't come to nice places like Poppleton. It isn't immediately practicable but it is something we should work toward rather than letting go of that aspiration and letting higher education be undermined as it is being at the moment. If we can't get it tomorrow it isn't an argument for accepting something less. It's a good argument for working with something less and for defending and extending it. It's elitist only in the sense that at present only some people are able to take advantage of it and I think getting away is an important part of it if people want to take advantage of that.

Such an ideal of extending unchanged higher education for a minority to a majority of the population justified resisting any change in the existing higher education experience of students. This was the position held by the majority of staff and students interviewed at Home Counties, like the law lecturer above. His opinion, bolstered by the ultra-left line of the Trotskyist groupuscule to which he belonged, implied that any acceptance of or adaptation to the new realities of more students without additional funding was seen as letting the side down. Such actions were regarded as setting the institution on the slippery slope towards becoming 'like a former-polytechnic' and so 'no longer a proper university', making the whole place like the despised Business School which yet provided so much of its funding through selling expensive courses to wealthy foreigners.

The minority of Home Counties staff who attempted such accommodations were castigated or, at best, superciliously regarded by the hard-line majority. That their dismissive views could be reciprocated is shown by the following 'soft' opinion expressed jokingly by an information scientist who declared that

> Compared with English and other useless subjects like sociology, we're in a better position than them. I can understand why they think as they do but they could always put on courses in spelling and grammar for our students!

This shows that some of the 'hard' nuts were not wrong to be suspicious of some of their 'soft' colleagues.

Aware of differences of opinion, many of the staff interviewed at Home Counties indicated that the options facing the institution in the new marketplace should be squarely faced by the collegiate body of staff who could then decide on the position to take:

> Then one could decide what kind of institution one wanted to be. As it is we seem to be just drifting before the government wind which keeps changing in direction and strength, like all the universities. Until we get to the position where we can face a possible choice between, say, would you rather be a small liberal arts college or a large university with all subjects, and if you were a liberal arts college, say, then you'll have to get a large number of students from overseas, so you'll be rather like a finishing school, a bit twee but well-founded with decent working conditions. Or would you rather be a second-rate generalist university?

From the way this interviewee posed this choice, it is clear what his preferred alternative would be and it is the impression of this study that it would be shared by the overwhelming majority of Home Counties staff.

At Inner City a similar division also constantly contested the future corporate identity of the institution in the marketplace. 'Soft' staff supported a continuation of the polytechnic ideal as originally established to be a service centre to local industry and the community from which it was intended to draw its students. They supported and were supported by entrepreneurial initiatives that led to employer participation in the institution and to a learner-managed learning framework for study and teaching. Funding for this approach came from the Department of Employment, via the Enterprise in Higher Education Initiative (see p. 81). A survey of staff involved in this Initiative indicated that it attracted those who already possessed some professional interest or qualification in pedagogy or human communication or counselling and guidance. Many had also been involved in the former-School for Independent Study.

The Enterprise in Higher Education Initiative introduced student centredness and employer participation simultaneously, on the assumption that both aims were necessarily complementary. However, evaluation of the Initiative at both institutions suggests that at neither place did it successfully establish the connection between innovation in teaching and learning within the institution and mechanisms for employer/education liaison. These latter were in any case rendered difficult due to recession and, at Home Counties, due to the lack of large local employers. More fundamentally though, the failure demonstrated that 'student centredness' as conceived by the 'soft' staff who entertained the notion, did not necessarily correspond, save in a minority of cases, with those same staff's notion of participation by employers with whom they often failed to make effective contact and use. This was due to misperceptions on both sides but was, we would suggest, fundamentally because 'student centredness' was given primacy over vocational relevance by the academic staff involved in Enterprise-funded projects.

'Hard' staff, who were more strongly and openly opposed to any vocational relevance or 'employer interference' – as they saw it – in higher education, favoured by contrast the autonomous development of faculties and disciplines on the traditional university model. Funding for their approach came via research grants from the Department for Education. This reliance upon rival sources of external funding was heightened by the devolution of budgetary powers to faculties that would predictably sustain the already divergent orientations and cultures in each faculty. Confused managerial goals had been accentuated by this internal disagreement and the ultimate outcome is unclear at the time of writing, though Inner City as a whole seems to be moving towards an imitation of the traditional universities whose name it now shares but perhaps in a necessarily populist version of what Halsey called 'elitist teaching'.

What is clear from these interviews with staff at these two contrasted higher education institutions is that the different academic disciplines develop different criteria for evaluating the capabilities or 'intelligence' of the students who apply to them. These same criteria are then deployed by staff in reaching their judgements of student performance. In other words, the staff are agents in constructing – through the processes of selection and assessment – the structural positions of their institutions in the newly defined hierarchy of competing universities and colleges. Not only staff but students also collude as agents in consolidating institutional identities which are socially distinctive.

We have argued in chapter two that whatever their subject of study and whichever institution they attended – even in two colleges as socially contrasted as Home Counties and Inner City – the graduates we interviewed gained a common academic culture of generalised, as opposed to vocational, knowledge. Whether this will continue to be the case as heightened social differentiation of institutions occurs between the widening poles of the new hierarchy of HEIs competing for students in the marketplace is a question we have already raised.

The effort of former-polytechnics like Inner City to compete with the established universities they have joined in the academic marketplace is aided and abetted by those staff who see it as in their self-interest and in accordance with their self-perceptions as lecturers and researchers rather than as teachers, or 'facilitators' in the new jargon. They want to regard their institution as a university in some traditional sense, rather than as a school or further education college. It is, however, an unequal competition to which the features that were distinctive of Inner City's polytechnic mission are in danger of being sacrificed.

One of the elements of the original orientation towards local students that has been lost already was the unique School for Independent Study which the college sustained previously for nearly 20 years. As it provides us with an example of the type of approach to higher education which we believe should be generalised to the entire further and higher education, and for that matter to the school and continuing education and training, system, we next examine it in some detail.

4

Independent Study

The School for Independent Study

The School for Independent Study was founded at the college we have called Inner City University in 1974. It began life as a way of getting local people as teachers into local schools, initially offering a two-year diploma in higher education, but later going on to degree and then postgraduate level courses outwith any particular subject specialisation. Its full story has been told elsewhere by Derek Robbins (see bibliography). In 1991 however, due to a combination of circumstances, the School was closed and Independent Study was devolved to the other six schools of the soon to be redesignated University. In these new circumstances Independent Study as such soon ceased to exist.

During its lifespan the School steered a variable course between the twin poles of academicism and vocationalism. Initially it set out to broaden progressive ideals for the polytechnics. As such, the former-polytechnic as a whole was identified with the effort to bring comprehensive higher education to local, working-class students and to replace the concept of the middle-class boarding school university with that of the urban community university. In place of the traditional university alliance between liberal and academic education, Inner City Polytechnic represented an alliance of liberal ideals for education with vocational service to its students and the communities from which they came. There was therefore, in its interpretation of the original ideal of polytechnic education, a notion of useful knowledge embodied in the various schools of the former-polytechnic which opposed the academic notion of the cultivation of knowledge supposedly for its own sake. Amongst the schools of Applied Biology, Applied Economics, Applied Philosophy and so on, Independent Study was established as a School in its own right.

The School for Independent Study however went further: not

only did it affirm the right of students to vocational information for the furtherance of their career aims and of service to local industry and to the community; it also asserted the independent ability of students to pursue knowledge, up to degree level and beyond, that was useful to them for whatever reason. Independent Study would thus cross the departmental frontiers imposed upon the totality of knowledge and practice by professional and vocational requirements on the one hand and academic specialisms and sub-specialisms on the other. It therefore went far beyond the supposedly innovative 'inter-disciplinarity' that was featured rather ostentatiously by the then 'new' universities of the 1960s, such as Home Counties.

As Halsey argued (see p. 45), this 'academic inter-disciplinarity' in fact represented nothing more than a rejection of the Victorian Civic university organisation of single subject degrees on the German model of professional organisation, in favour of a return to the Oxbridge tradition of gentlemanly cultural cultivation in multisubject schools. Certainly, Home Counties' interdisciplinarity had been the result of a refinement of course content carried out by academics without reference to any perception of what their likely future students might bring to that content or derive from it. It reflected an academic view of course design in which subjects represented discrete bodies of knowledge to be handed down unchanged to the future generations of students from whom would be selected the successors to donnish dominion.

Instead, Independent Study required its students to identify a field of special interest to them which was seen as a vehicle for developing the generalised knowledge and higher level cognitive skills of logical thinking and rational argument of working-class people – beyond the level of narrow vocational knowledge previously considered necessary to complete their productive labour. They would thus make sense of and generalise their own experience to become familiar with a different way of thinking that was otherwise the exclusive prerogative of society's rulers, or of those who ruled on their behalf. By this means, as we said earlier, the totality of known facts relevant to their particular chosen subject could be acquired and ordered logically and scientifically for their own benefit. In this case, as it was originally formulated, students would use this knowledge as teachers for the benefit of their own social class, whose children they would teach to think in like manner.

Independent Study, however, soon moved on from this rather patronising attempt to facilitate the self-improvement and mental self-emancipation of the local working class. It emphasised, through the part which students played in devising their own courses of study, a recognition of the need for people's active participation in the construction of their own social institutions and environments. There was therefore an essential democratic component to the work of the School. As one of its founding declarations of intent stated:

> Democracy requires political competence of a high order. If power is to be shared people need to know how to use it! They need to know how social institutions work and how they can be changed. This sort of competence has to be learnt.

This competence was, moreover, not a final end state to be reached by students but a developing capacity which is acquired as it is exercised. Education was thus recognised as an essentially open-ended process that was inherently unpredictable so that its results could not be anticipated by either teachers or learners. As the document went on,

> The logic of discovery is consistent with educational principle. The first and most difficult task is to formulate problems; the second to propound trial solutions; the third to test these solutions with rigour. It is this framework which enables students to take the responsibility we assign to them [of developing their own course design], and gives a guarantee that the process is an educative one. We rely, in short, less on content than on method.

Education was therefore seen not as a passive process of transmitting knowledge but as an active process of self-directed enquiry following rational and scientific method.

If this was the somewhat idealistic original conception of Independent Study, it did not, needless to say, work out like that in practice. The emphasis of the original diploma on method rather than content, and competence rather than knowledge, was generally unacceptable and incomprehensible not only to the academic authorities validating the qualification but also to the students themselves. They quickly perceived that such a course was not going to receive significant national recognition for them to be able to pursue their own careers beyond a circumscribed vocational ghetto. Independent Study thus came to offer an alternative rather than a substitute way of learning. Nevertheless, by the late 1980s the School accounted for nearly one in ten of the then-polytechnic's total enrolment.

By that time however, an historical sea-change had occurred. The language of progressive education upon which the original submission for the School for Independent Study had been based was subverted. It was appropriated by the Manpower Services Commission, a new state agency, set up in 1974 to deal with the labour problems arising from the restructuring of the economy, and from widening and structural mass unemployment in particular. The MSC turned the progressive critique of existing academic education, which pointed out its irrelevance to real life, into the justifications for a new economic rationalisation where what came to be known as 'the new vocationalism' of education found its relevance in the needs of industry. 'The world of work' was thus presented as the unproblematic and natural arena in which individuals could find self-fulfilment and achieve 'vocational maturity'.

The progressive educationalists behind the School for Independent Study naturally did not wish to collaborate in the Labour government's 1976 renunciation of its comprehensive education policy that was marked by Prime Minister Callaghan's Ruskin speech – especially when the subsequent Thatcher government appropriated this new vocationalism for its assault upon comprehensive education. The School for Independent Study therefore more or less unconsciously redefined 'competence', the central term of both progressive anti-academicism and the new vocationalism, away from the MSC's notion of 'vocational competence' towards competence as personal independence. By thus concentrating on developing the capacity of students to act rather than to study independently, rationality was devalued. The subsequent neglect of objective learning tended to reduce educational processes to the level of assertion training. The mistake made by educational progressives here was to identify an attack on academicism with an attack on intellectuality.

This was a common failing of much oppositional educational reform which, throughout the 1960s and 1970s, branded intellectual rigour and integrity as elitist along with academicism. Yet it was surely right to assert that the opportunity to think and reflect should not be the preserve of a sponsored minority group of 'academics'. The campaign by academics for intellectual freedom, against the incursions, first, of the vocationalising and, then, the marketising efforts of central state intervention in education, has been a campaign for their own freedom, the freedom of academic inquiry. They claim that this benefits the whole of society but, as long as universities remain elite institutions, this claim rings rather hollow. Instead, we need to create the conditions which allow everyone – not just a chosen few academics – the opportunity freely to develop and exercise their intellectual powers. If society is indeed undergoing a knowledge revolution and if, therefore, knowledge is power, a renewed commitment by educationists to the advancement of the democratic intellect offers hope for the empowerment of the oppressed.

This empowerment was the original promise of Independent Study, but in the end the School fell victim to the battle in higher education between the collegiate and hierarchical models of management. In this battle for the soul of the institution, 'hard'-line staff, with a conception of themselves and of the subjects that they teach derived from their own traditional university educations, have allied themselves with the collegiate ideal of a traditional university. The illusions of collegiality have been sustained by the devolution of funding to departmental cost centres which gives many of them access for the first time to limited research funding from the Department for Education. On the other hand, 'soft'-centred staff have allied themselves with what was one of the final flings of the vocational phase of education policy, the Department of Employment's Enterprise in Higher Education Initiative (see p. 81). At Inner City this took as its definition of enterprise Independent Study for all students in a learner-managed learning framework for study and teaching. As Independent Study was now to be everywhere in the form of enterprise, it was no longer required to be anywhere in particular and this provided the rationale for closing the School for Independent Study in July 1991, though there were other factors also involved (see pp. 134 and 139).

So at the time of interviewing students for this study in the summer of 1991 it became apparent that, among other things, their comments would provide an obituary for Independent Study. Let them now therefore explain the processes and benefits of Independent Study in their own words. We can then go on to judge how far the positive experiences of Independent Study at Inner City offer a way forward for all students in the education of the future.

The origins of psychotherapy, holography, child abuse, stage-lighting and journalism

In one sense you can see Independent Study as being closer to the older classical form of university education that existed in Europe, at the time when Marx was a student for example, in the sense that in that time people could structure pretty freely their own approach, their own style to what they were trying to say, without constraints from other so-called disciplines – and 'discipline' might be a telling word there. I suppose, if you look at Marx as a classic case, he started out studying jurisprudence and through his study of that it led him on to the study of economics. What that says to me is that the creative functions were looked upon more openly in those days. If you like, the products of mind were less constrained by rule systems. Now I see Independent Study as having some of this kind of quality whereby people can be more creative in their approaches to their work and in that express their own meaning a bit more accurately, a bit more freely – freely is probably a better word. It's a different approach to – what shall we say? – 'problem solving'. It's more to do with developing the intellectual potential of the human brain.

This 59 year-old student's subject of study was the origins of psychotherapy. After a lifetime of travelling and working around the world as a merchant seaman:

All the time I continued with my personal reading and eventually I decided just to do something about it in terms of finding some kind of formalisation of my thoughts and ideas and that's what led me into higher education... I was living locally and I personally admired what the School for Independent Study was doing. I found that I couldn't do this kind of study anywhere else and I was disappointed with the world of – shall we say? – established psychiatry and I thought that I would like to continue a stream of thought that went back to Freud and started all over again.

John's study thus related to a dispute that was then current in psychoanalytic circles, as to whether Freud reformulated his theory in the light of the criticism it received and the social ostracism that he faced after his first lecture to the psychological society of Vienna in 1895. John's conclusion, written up in a dissertation upon which he had been examined, and which might then be commercially published, was that:

I think Freud was a victim of his own suggestion and of his times and circumstances, but he was a revolutionary and our understanding of the world today is different because of him.

This knowledge was not however a purely academic conclusion:

> Could I put it this way? – that not only myself but most people who
> enter higher education have a body of knowledge that they need to
> formalise in some way. You need to put it into a different context so
> that it can be put into a practical useful mode if you like. That's what
> I did, so that I am now in the process of starting my own consultancy
> in hypnosis and analysis. I've also done training as well. I'm not doing
> what I'm doing just on the basis of a degree in Independent Study.

However as a result of the degree:

> I acquired the skills of listening deeply – listening more than saying,
> because if you really want to understand what someone is saying you
> really have to listen carefully. It's called active listening in the world of
> counselling. I also think differently, particularly in the sense that when
> I speak to people I feel myself being more precise about the commu-
> nication of my meaning to them. I mean that in the sense of not just
> being pedantic, you know, because the pedant will just go on and on.
> I also acquired the knack of presenting academic findings – how to
> structure your communication in such a way that someone else can
> understand it. That's an intellectual skill really.

Another student, Alice, was also from a working-class background and lived locally. She was 28 and had worked as a secretary
before getting married and having two young children. One of
the offices at which she had been employed was in a company
making holograms and she became interested in the subject of
holography.

> I saw a gap in terms of what kind of holograms are being made for
> commercial production. I thought there was room for more tailor-made
> models for holograms, art holograms more than anything else – things
> people would buy to put on their wall. Also, to use holography as part
> of other designs as well – a 3D holograph to fit in with a 2D element.
> I think there is a potential here for development in advertising.

She therefore approached the college with her idea and a learning
contract was drawn up.

> The things that I wanted to do weren't available anywhere else. That
> was one of the criteria for getting onto IS.

For her part, Alice had to be sure that the college could provide
the expertise and facilities that she would need. This was
problematic, not only in terms of the resources and time that the
college would have to make available.

I had problems getting specialised information from the physics department. They wanted to restrict access to their specialised information. One lecturer actually put a book on a table with a boomp! and said, 'You have to learn maths to this level to understand anything. You IS students come here expecting the earth!' He was visibly annoyed with me for not being a student on his course. I quoted Einstein at him: 'If an expert can't tell a layman what he does in five minutes then he's not an expert.' He was not pleased at all, but... another lecturer in physics was prepared to set up a holographic studio to help me. He was really excited about it. I was also in touch with some of the leading authorities in the field at Leicester University.

For their part, the college tutors had to be sure that Alice would be able to complete the study once it was begun and that it would meet the criteria for degree-level investigation.

I showed them my qualifications which weren't that much – three 'O' levels – but they based it on an interview with the art and design course tutor who became my specialist tutor. I did the two-year diploma first. [After that] the pre-degree course was very demanding; the proposal that you had to put to the CNAA was quite strict. You had to satisfy their demands.

As part of the course I worked at Laser Light Works holographic studio through one summer holiday. I was a holographer's assistant really. That's where I learnt a lot of the skills for making holograms and produced some of my own holograms there as well. The technical skills I acquired were twofold: firstly, in relation to making the holograms themselves and, secondly, in adapting existing artistic skills to making the models for holography. So you've got the actual technical skills of making holograms and the creative, practical skills that have been honed towards making models for holograms.

In sum,

It's given me a chance to do other things other than be a secretary or a filing assistant.

But also,

The approach to creative skills has become much more self-disciplined. In all areas, not just creative stuff, but other things as well. Say I wanted to study guitar or something, I could apply those learning skills to doing it. Using my own method that you've developed yourself rather than having a method that you've had thrust upon you... Elements of your character that you don't naturally have that you develop, like patience and persistence. That's really helped me a lot in all sorts of things.

The emphasis upon being able to study in their own way was repeated by a number of Independent Study students whose previous educational experiences had not been happy ones. As one student said,

> Practically everybody at the School for Independent Study has had really bad experiences with education and it gives them an opportunity to overcome those by really studying for themselves.

Independent Study, as another student described it,

> It's a different ball-game altogether because they don't fit into a mould. They tend to think independently and they don't fit into what is considered normal.

For example, a 31 year-old recalled how

> Education didn't suit me as a younger person. I never learnt how to play the game basically... I don't know if IS suits mature people more but I think an 18 year-old would have more difficulty because they've just come out of an institution that tells them what to do, whereas I think it suited my nature to find out the answers to my questions myself.

Similarly, her younger sister thought,

> I've learnt and I will remember much more than I would have done on a conventional course 'cos a lot of conventional courses you've just got to remember for an exam and if you've got that kind of memory you're OK. I didn't have an exam for my degree. I did a dissertation and it's all based on course work and then you write a review saying how you learnt things and what you'd do differently; you evaluate your own work... I've also learnt a lot from the other students. You do seminar papers so you learn a lot even if it's a completely different subject from what you're doing. It's aimed to help their study – you discuss how they could have done it better but you learn about their subject as well.

It was not unusual for students to be related and indeed one married couple were interviewed together. Maggie and Frank were 47, their children had left their council home and they were unemployed when they started their course.

> I always wanted to go on with education... Even while I was in the army I did courses. I think education is very important. I think our generation is more education conscious than our parents were. I went to a Restart course that the Job Centre had sent me on. It was only one week but the woman who was running it asked me if I'd ever thought of doing a DipHE 'cos she'd done one herself. 'Cos what it

was, I'd been unemployed and I asked if there was any course to do with stage lighting and she told me the only way I could get on it was through the School for Independent Study.

This then brought his wife in:

Well, really, it was just the fact that Frank started in September and I started going to the student clubs and that and the students started talking me into it.

I said to her, 'You don't want to stay at home all the time now the kids are off your hands.'

Frank first got involved in theatre through being social secretary of the tenants' association club

and that was the first time in my life that I'd really found something that did interest me.

Maggie's subject of study was child abuse,

Probably because of bringing up six children it was the most practical one to go into. Child abuse wasn't what I started off looking into, but it was later because there's a lot of families around here – just in this little square alone – who've had their children taken away from them. So I thought when I do get qualified I'll have the qualifications in that area 'cos they're crying out for social workers in that area.

FRANK: It's an experience I'm glad I've done – very rewarding. Also I've picked up so many other things, nothing to do with my course. I mean students – a lot of people have got funny ideas about them – and through being one I know that isn't true.

MAGGIE: The same as Frank says, you learn things that you never thought you would and you meet people from different walks of life.

FRANK: You find you're a lot more prepared to help people on that course...

MAGGIE: We've actually had students come round and sit down here and sort things out with us... You do get a lot of satisfaction from it. When you've got that work done and all bound up in a book then you feel you've achieved something.

FRANK: Mind you, people say, 'It's only a bit of paper', but I say 'It's what that bit of paper represents' [because] I've got enough knowledge that I could go and teach somebody who knows nothing about my subject, I could teach them it in theory. I am now able to get hold of a technical subject like mine and explain it in layman's terms where anybody could pick it up and I think a lot of the students, especially the older ones, have gone into tutoring. In fact, I would say that it is a teachers' course in a way.

MAGGIE: It gives you confidence in yourself, which I did lack before I started the course.

FRANK: It gives you the confidence to stand up and explain your subject to other people.

MAGGIE: I used to shake from head to foot. You could see the paper shaking in my hand. But I did it.

We would not wish to give the impression that the students of IS were exclusively and traditionally working-class in origin however, although admission to the School required no formal qualifications, but demanded only, as one student related, 'a clear idea of what you wanted to study and why you wanted to study it'.

Indeed, one Danish student of 29 had, as she said, 'the equivalent of 'A' levels and 'O' levels in Denmark':

I was brought up in a middle-class environment, there's no doubt about that... I was on what they call the student exam course that would take you on to university in Denmark but I bumped into my husband in the meantime and moved over here. I was thinking of journalism school in Denmark but it's very difficult to get in there but I had always planned to go.

So when she heard about Independent Study while modelling at the Fine Art School,

That was the perfect solution as a student for me... Independent Study has always seemed to me the ideal way for a mature student to get into education again because sitting with a class of 16 year-olds is not a very attractive idea for a 25 year-old; it's a different mentality altogether. But more importantly, I find the older you get, the more focused you get in your aims and you don't have to tag along with a load of things that are not going to be beneficial for you.

I found that, well, first of all, obviously, since you have to focus your study, my focus of study I know much more about, which was the privatisation of the waterboards – that's an excuse for studying the field of communications, the media's treatment of water privatisation, and that was fantastic. It was so interesting, but within that I had to go through four disciplines – sociology, economics, politics and communications, theories of all four disciplines that I had to go through in my dissertation. I was lucky my tutor had all four disciplines and was professor of this and 'Blah-Blah' in all these things – a very qualified man. So I really find that it's widened my knowledge on all of those areas enormously but, perhaps most importantly, I find that because IS doesn't teach you so much a specific knowledge, it teaches you how to gain knowledge, that's what it teaches you and that's the most important thing in journalism, how to gain knowledge on your own account, off your own back and I've learnt that, that's for sure.

IS is a very draining process. You've really got to have your head wrapped around what you're trying to do. Compared with younger people – they're so sort of conditioned from school and everything, their choice of study is dictated by their parents and teachers and they have a very strict discipline to sit through lectures and so on. They don't have the same scope for a personal interpretation of the world, let's put it that way. What it has to do with is children from the age of five being told to stand in line and right through their lives do what they're told and that is what is wrong with English culture. The only way to change anything in the education system is to have people ask questions. Ask questions again and again. That's the only way you educate people. So I think the real reason for closing the School for Independent Study was that, however much the government might say they want education for a wider audience, they still put in obstacles to stop that because, when you have mature people studying what they want, there is a real danger that people really start to think.

Self-development, parapsychology, astrology and crystals

It was not the subversive potential of the School that provided the rationale for its closure however. The subjects of study were, an interviewee explained, 'mostly to do with education and social work and sometimes art and design.' One IS student interviewed had indeed studied 'The Economic Underdevelopment of the Third World by Western Imperialism' – a subject she later published a book about; and another, who subsequently went to work in a local authority women's equality unit, studied 'The History of Women's Equality Units and the Management of Women's Self-Help Groups in the UK'. These were perfectly legitimate subjects for study however.

There were obviously resource and staffing problems in the School, which with its system of individual and group tutorials was very labour intensive. It was also evident, from many of the interviews with IS students, that in the group-work sessions that were built into all the individually negotiated courses, so as not to leave students completely on their own but to learn from other students and to encourage team-working and other so-called 'personal and transferable skills', many students were being put through hoops by some staff who followed their own particular variants of group-working psychology. The games-playing and other 'touchy-feely' group activities were evidently resented by some IS students interviewed, though all valued the study skills sessions and most appreciated the mixed groups at which 'you had to explain what you were doing to other people who didn't know anything about it', so 'you learnt what other people were doing'.

These difficulties were exacerbated by the low esteem in which academically 'hard' members of staff elsewhere in the institution held the 'soft' IS. These perceptions were not lost on the IS students interviewed. For instance,

> I feel that IS is looked down upon by the other departments. They feel it's not conventional study, like sitting down to lectures and studying, but I feel that IS can be a lot harder than doing it the conventional way but then these other things give it a bad name.

'These other things' were the immediate problems that led to the School's closure and they were revealed in a number of the interviews, as well as being instanced by one particular student interviewee who had taken himself as his subject of study. When he thought that he knew enough about himself, he had left his study in his second year without even taking the Diploma, to join a pyramid-selling organisation. This was conceived by the interviewee more as a religious organisation dedicated to the continuing self-realisation of himself and those he persuaded to join him, than as a vehicle for the profits that his activities generated for the organisation's US backers.

> I signed on to study acupuncture, but when I got there I realised the potential of Independent Study and it totally changed my life. My life was changing anyway but my personal tutor kept talking about self-awareness in the groups they had and suddenly something clicked in me and I found what I'd been looking for all my life if you like. I was looking externally but I realised I should've looked inside of me and I got a specialist tutor who was very much into personal growth and Carl Rogers and he gave me a book [by Rogers] that changed my life as well. But what I was studying wasn't the main focus of it any more. I became the focus.

This ellipsis of meaning, veering away from any predefined object of study, whether within traditional academic divisions or by the negotiation leading to contract and registration for independent study, shows the danger of 'experiential learning', 'self-managed learning', 'contract learning', and individual and person-centred educational reform generally. The response to these dangers, however, must be more than to fall back upon academic traditionalism. For that response too would not get to the heart of contemporary anti-intellectualism and irrationality.

From Alice's point of view,

> It's a pity that there are so many people doing things like parapsychology, astrology and other 'new wave' things like that – crystals! If I hear that word again, I'll scream! Mind you, that is mostly at the Diploma level; they don't get through to the degree. If it all got like that, they might as well close it down.'

Other interviewees, too, queried this kind of course:

> With astrology and things like that you can't help wondering, how did they find the tutors for them!

Or, as John put it in his measured tones,

> There's a peculiar question of academic freedom that needs to be addressed here because I found it a bit difficult sometimes to make sense of some people spending the period of a degree study on the subject of astrology. Now this in my opinion did not seem to contribute a great deal to the community at large. It crossed more into the realm of simplistic belief systems rather than anything that could be scientifically supported. It's a question of science but in the end what it amounts to is values and beliefs, which throws us into the political world whether we like it or not.

These are indeed profound political and philosophical problems which go to the root of the contemporary battle being waged throughout higher education today, for and against academic freedom to study for its own sake, and between different conceptions of what is really useful knowledge. In this battle, as exemplified in the two contrasted higher education institutions we have examined, staff have been seen to be divided between 'hard' and 'soft' positions allied to two different conceptions of higher education. One is represented by traditional academia and supported by educational traditionalists in the Department for Education and the other by a version of polytechnic education allied to the vocational aims of the Department of Employment.

In the market place in students established by the latest education reforms, the worst of both worlds could well result – elite and vocationally irrelevant but socially prestigious academic education for a few, combined in various proportions with vocationally related and intellectually inferior courses for the mass of students. Then elite higher education will predictably cling to its traditional course organisation of organically accumulated information and knowledge, while mass higher education will embrace modular course forms as means to increase access and to empower students to acquire vocational competences.

Before going on to outline an alternative to these two opposed camps of 'hardline' academicism versus 'soft' and student-centred vocationalism, we turn briefly to a consideration of the modularity which the 'hardline' staff interviewed at both Inner City and Home Counties saw as subversive of traditional higher education.

Modularity

Modularity is a half-way house between traditionally cumulative academic courses of study within habitually defined disciplines, and independent study, to whatever level of research, experiment or creation, in an individually negotiated but nevertheless objectively real subject of study. Individual students following a modular degree programme can also construct their own courses but only from the modules or units on offer. Modularity was therefore rejected as an alternative in the original proposal for a degree by Independent Study because:

> inter-disciplinary or modular approaches to course design simply reinforce the 'top-down' attitudes to which higher education generally conforms'.

In this traditional hierarchy,

> The department presupposes an organised body of knowledge, which is understood by some people (professors, and to a decreasing extent assistant professors and lecturers of various grades) and passed on to others.

Interdisciplinarity in its revived guise at the new universities of the 1960s or in its modern form of modularisation ostensibly breaks up the department. However, by the organisation of prerequisite 'pathways', even though they allow of 'elective', 'additional' – or, as at Home Counties, 'wild' – courses or modules, traditional departments can maintain their hold upon their students. This is the reason that modularity, in the form of re-naming all units of study as modules, was so readily accepted – even by 'hardline' staff – at Home Counties, who changed the names only to remain the same.

For, as the Independent Study proposal pointed out, whether in interdisciplinary choice of units or in fully modularised courses, even though students have a wide choice of options available,

> The teachers possess the power, and the students do not. The teachers determine what the subject is and how it shall be presented. They arrange, before the students arrive, the course, the curriculum, syllabuses, and the detail of timetables. The students must take it or leave it.

This was not enough for the proposers of Independent Study who argued instead that

> It is possible to enable students to create their own programmes of higher education, to offer this opportunity to most people whether or not they have done well in the education service in the past, and to be, in short, a genuine service to the community. The programme differs from others in higher education in that it is based, not upon subject disciplines or upon combinations of subjects, but upon the logic of learning. It is this which gives the programme its coherence and the students an assurance of its value.

It enables staff to give students responsibility not just

> for selecting 'options' but for planning their own programmes. It will be for students to formulate and agree their goals with staff and peers, their methods of reaching them and the means of testing their performance.

This would thus go beyond the freedom, which many students already exercise, of holding different opinions from their teachers, the expression of which is indeed encouraged, especially in the arts and social sciences. Yet a student's opinion in a seminar can never be as valid as that of the seminar leader because it can rarely go so far as to challenge the basic premises of the subject, about what is and what is not worth studying, or how it should be studied. This was what it was proposed Independent Study would do, really 'empowering' students in a genuine dialogue of equals with staff. This went beyond offering them consumer choice from the range of modules handed down to them from on high.

Moreover, as has been seen in the descriptions by staff of the modules they offered in engineering and business studies at Inner City, as well as in history and information science at Home Counties, modular course design involves specifying the outcomes of study in advance.

Another danger, which 'hardliners' were quick to point out, is that this can lead to a commodification of knowledge, with a reduction from knowledge as process to knowledge as prepackaged product. Then, in place of engagement with a traditional discipline, the body of knowledge and information so defined would be subdivided into modules for easy digestion by the student as consumer banking accumulated credit points. A market in modules could well pander both to faddish intellectual consumerism and vocational preference as determined by labour market value – 'interesting' modules being combined with 'useful' ones. In the process, general level knowledge or meta-knowledge – what we have called knowledge of rules about rules, and the ability to deal with information rather than memorisation of bits of information – could be lost.

Advocates of the modular approach suggest that such higher level knowledge would be more effectively and deliberately developed through the process of negotiating a modular programme during which students would have to relate modules from one area to those in another. This offers, as one advocate wrote at Inner City, 'citizenship of a pluralistic intellectual domain' in place of 'cultural assimilation into an academicised elite'. He hoped therefore

> that the new forms of learning will create new forms of student interaction and cohesion to replace the fading collegiality of the old elite culture.

In addition, he pointed out that student outcomes were just as predictable (to staff at least) in traditional degrees, though they were not made explicit to students following these courses.

In Independent Study, by contrast, outcomes were essentially unpredictable, although the methods of reaching them were guaranteed by the learning contract between student and institution. On the basis of our interviews with students who completed their Independent Study to degree level, we have suggested that their study had developed the same critical, general level, so-called 'higher cognitive' skills of reasoning and logical or scientific thinking that were common to the shared academic culture of generalised, as opposed to vocational, knowledge that students had gained in traditional subject disciplines at whichever institution they attended.

However, our interviewees – both staff and students at Inner City – had also commented on the more demanding nature of Independent Study for those who took it seriously. This, they said, made it more appropriate for adult students, who, as one of them stated above, had 'really got their heads wrapped around what they were trying to do'. Indeed, the youngest Independent Studies student interviewed was 23 and the oldest 59, with most being in their 30s and 40s, and the original submission for the diploma quoted above envisaged Independent Study as an extension of the then-polytechnic's adult programme.

For most younger students more support was thought necessary, and to extend to them the benefits of access and flexibility that made Independent Study so attractive to mature entrants, a modular DipHE was introduced in 1983. This allowed students a choice of modules from half of the various subject areas then available in the polytechnic. Later – similarly to the development of the SIS – this was topped up to degree level and then integrated in a combined studies programme. Its flexibility – allowing part-time study of only one or two modules, or stopping at various points – was particularly attractive to mature students for whom this flexibility had also been part of the attraction of Independent Study. The modular degree, as it became known, soon attracted up to 25 per cent of all undergraduate entrants, taking students away from Independent Study and providing another reason for its demise. Modularity was then generalised in 1993 to all subjects of study and, simultaneously, two module-length semesters spread over three terms were also introduced. All students now study three modules per semester, six modules per year, on the pattern which is becoming increasingly familiar in the mass further and higher education system as it is now developing in England and Wales. All new applicants therefore apply for one, two, or, at most, three subjects in various combinations of major, major and minor, or joint two or three subject qualifications.

In a typical system, like the one that was subsequently adopted when the modular degree was generalised to all subjects of study at Inner City, each module is assessed at the end of each semester out of 20 grade points. Students can thus gain a maximum 120 points per year. It is immaterial whether or not it actually takes them a calendar year to accumulate the required pass out of 120. A student might follow an accelerated course (over three semesters in a year if a trimester is added over the summer, for instance), or be accredited for one or more modules by prior experience, to complete in less than a year; or, contrariwise, a student could take up to three years to take two modules per half semester – longer if they re-sat them. They could do similarly in subsequent 'years', enabling part-time as well as accelerated study.

The first year's pass out of a total of 120 equals certificate level, or part one of a degree, qualifying the student to continue to a more specialised part two. The second year (out of an accumulated total of 240) is then equivalent to Higher National Diploma level, while the third year (out of a final total of 360) gains a degree. One of the effects of modularisation, and of accompanying systems of credit accumulation and transfer is to solidify this, already implicit, ordering of qualifications. It thus provides a number of exit points, reducing, so its proponents argue, the stigma of failure for students who do not stay the whole course. This system of credit accumulation is thus independent of the divisions associated with the honours system but could be made coterminous with them.

It could also lead towards the development of American-type transcript documents. These records of a student's achievement are well understood by employers as well as by students in North America, who typically strive to keep up their 'grade point average' as they progress through their courses. Critics argue that this leads to instrumental attitudes among students, who become obsessed with their current average mark at the expense of interest in and enthusiasm for the subject as well as idealism for its professional application. This is a frequent criticism also of undergraduate education in Sweden where students similarly study a sequence of courses that add up to a degree. Many Swedish students supposedly tick off units as they successfully complete them, forgetting, instead of integrating and recapitulating, the knowledge and skills that they acquired along the way. (However, this also happens in traditionally academic courses, not only to degree level. Everything is recalled for the examination and forgotten thereafter.)

Transcripts could however go beyond grade points as, with students increasingly following diverse trajectories or even individual learning packages, broad norm-referenced assessments will have to be replaced by detailed criterion-referenced transcripts. However, except in certain specialised areas – usually associated with art, the media and fashion, where students create portfolios of their work to show prospective employers – employers are not unduly interested in the finer details of their graduate applicants' degree programmes. At least initially, as a screening device, employers only require a simple grade they can understand to sort out applicants for interview. At interview, the transcript, record of achievement or portfolio might then provide the interviewer with something to talk to the applicant about. Just as for school leavers, it was quickly understood by employers that a C grade in GCSE was the respectable pass mark no matter how good a 'Record of Achievement' the pupil had compiled whilst at school.

In the American model of higher education curriculum, a first-year foundation course (sometimes franchised to associated further education or community colleges – as they are known there) often lays the basis for the more narrow choice of subject(s) to be taken in subsequent years. The first year then becomes a period in which, through the selection of appropriate modules, the key competencies are developed to permit more independent work in the second and third years – thus saving on staff time and coping with larger numbers of students. It is said that many US students who are not suited to higher studies are 'cooled out' of the system at this stage. However, as well as 'cooling out', there may also be a tendency to 'drift up' the system during an extended period of further education. In any case, this idea of a preliminary induction to further study is also the intention of a foundation year for certain traditional degree courses, like some of those at Home Counties.

Other proponents of the American system – like the Home Counties professor of history interviewed in the last chapter – argue for specialisation later still. Then the whole modularised first degree becomes preparatory for specialisation at postgraduate, Masters level, when, as the professor said, 'it's law or whatever as it ever was'. This would be compatible with the suggested 'two-plus-two-plus-two' – 2 years certificate, 2 years degree, 2 years masters – system of qualification. In this system the normal progression for 16 year-old school leavers would be that the first two years of study for a national certificate or baccalaureate combining 'academic' and vocational modules at NVQ level three, would be spent in further education. Students would then move on at 18-plus to a two-year degree (equals NVQ4). This in turn would qualify them for a specialised two-year postgraduate Master's programme (NVQ5). Such a scheme also fitted with the history professor's and many other interviewees' opinion – both those who approved it and those who did not – that 'we're moving in the American direction'.

The American system of elective choice has been part of a mass higher education since American colleges and universities broke with the European tradition of heavily specialised unilinear courses in the early nineteenth century. In England by comparison, as reflected in our interviews with 'hardline' staff at both Inner City and Home Counties, mass higher education is still regarded by many academics as a contradiction in terms. This was primarily because higher education was regarded by them as essentially an individual process. Small groups, if not one-to-one tutorials, were therefore essential and it could not be envisaged how, without exorbitant funding, such intimate contact could be retained in a mass system. As a Home Counties biologist put it,

> I think you genuinely do need the small group teaching to discuss the crazy ideas students may have because it doesn't matter if they're crazy as long as they're discussing them.

Proponents of mass higher education accepted this but offered alternative means of supplying the personal element – from tutorial support in modular schemes to replacing the person of the teacher by that of the fellow student, as in peer tutoring (students on the same course learning together) and student mentoring (second and third years teaching first and second years).

From our point of view, irrespective of the numbers involved, the crucial question is whether a modular degree can develop the same level of more open generalised, as opposed to closed vocational, knowledge as was developed by traditional degree level study. Whether, in terms we have used earlier, the knowledge – and knowledge about knowledge – that students gain from their degree level education is open to the same level of explanation and determination as was shared previously by the common academic culture of traditional degree courses. We have argued that this existed across the binary divide between the old university and polytechnic higher education system. Will the social polarity that always existed in the binary system, but which is now arguably being aggravated by the rapid expansion of higher education, be complemented by a division, accentuated by modularisation and semesterisation, within the previously unitary academic culture of higher education?

Elite or Ivy League universities will persist, we have predicted, in traditional degree courses, and will resist modularisation and semesterisation, so making transfer of credit accumulated elsewhere very difficult if not practically impossible. Instead, they will continue selectively to recruit their students from their traditionally associated private and more-or-less grammar/opted-out and grant maintained schools. Moreover, the traditional degrees that such traditional universities offer will continue to be socially prestigious and enjoy the same advantages as ever in the graduate labour market. By comparison with them, will the modular higher education of the mass of 'lesser' universities and colleges now – and we would argue for the first time – be academically worth less?

This question can be put another way. Just because modules offer intellectual outcomes that are made explicit, does this mean that the level of generalised knowledge acquired by their students cannot add up as a whole to equal the organically accumulated but inexplicit outcomes of traditional specialist discipline degrees? Both, after all, are 'closed' at a certain level decided in advance by their teachers. Only Independent Study offers the opportunity of going beyond this determination to genuinely new and possibly more open and higher levels of learning, discovery and creation.

On the basis of our – admittedly limited – number of interviews with graduates of the then-modular degree at Inner City, we would argue that modular degree courses need not necessarily result in a loss of general level knowledge and a restriction to vocationally specific and intellectually limited competences specified explicitly in advance. However, modular courses of study need to be carefully organised and supported by staff, especially if they are to create the sense of belonging corresponding to that of apprenticeship in an academic discipline, as a way of developing that same general level of knowledge. Students need guidance through modules that build upon successive units, reinforcing and recapitulating knowledge and skills to create an organic whole equivalent to that provided by a traditional discipline which is greater than the sum of its parts. This requires additional staff time and resources, but these are not usually forthcoming. Without this additional investment, it will be difficult to create new 'academic homes' to give all students following modularised curricula the equivalent of disciplinary identities, as Inner City now intended.

The modular degree at Inner City

At the time of our interviews with students, four out of the fifty Inner City interviewees followed the then modular or combined studies degree scheme, as it was officially called. These four women, like the Independent Study students interviewed, were also older than average (24, 35, 37 and 46) and had studied different combinations of the modular courses then available. As one of them explained her degree, 'It's not in anything, no one subject. It's all different subjects.' So that, she added jokingly, 'I know it all, I do!'

Nevertheless all the modular degree students interviewed had centred their units of study around particular areas, except for one who had done a combined degree made up of modules from two subject areas. (One other interviewee had combined three areas in her last year, but as these were film studies and English literature, together with an Independent Study project in which she wrote and later went on to produce and direct, her own play, the modules made up a common area of study.)

As Janice, one of these students, explained,

> I started off doing sociology and Third World studies and linguistics because I wasn't sure of the area I wanted to go into. That's the flexibility of a modular degree – you can change. Two friends I studied with decided to drop the other subjects and do sociology straight, but my best friend like me concentrated on the Third World 'cos in the first year most people aren't very sure what they want to do. In the end I was majoring in Third world studies but in the beginning you're allowed to do six subjects and then in the second year you're allowed to drop one set, so I dropped linguistics and I did popular culture still with the sociology and the Third World studies, so by the end all my subjects were Third World related.

As a result, unlike most other Inner City and Home Counties traditional single honours degree students, Janice did not feel that she had acquired expertise in a particular area, save that of her dissertation on the pharmaceutical industry in the Third World, 'so I feel as though I have special knowledge of that.' She had also acquired the much mentioned 'confidence' that it has been seen was emphasised by many of the graduates interviewed. Partly, it seemed as if this had been gained as a result of negotiating her way through the complexities of the modular programme:

> In the first two years I was just studying the whole time. I felt like my whole life was round the college but this year it's been more relaxed. I think maybe the confidence grows. By the third year you think you understand what you're doing. A lot of people say, 'Isn't it confusing doing the modular degree?' but I like it 'cos if you're doing sociology and you get bored with it you can turn over and do something else, whereas if you're doing just straight economics it must get really tedious.

This flexibility of the modular degree which she had enjoyed was also valued as extending to other areas of her life. For instance, in the year's voluntary work that she had obtained, not in the Third world but with refugees from it in the USA,

> You do a month's training in Miami then you decide on your area of interest, so it's quite flexible. I'm used to that. I don't mind where I end up actually.

In her personal life too, asked if there would be conflicts between her own career aims and those of her partner, she replied, 'It would need flexibility on both sides.'

This might only have been coincidence, but when asked whether her thinking had changed as a result of her course of study – the question that usually elicited evidence of a different level of general cognition open to higher levels of determination – Janice answered that

> My politics have changed completely. I'm far more liberal minded.

Like other working-class students, this brought her into conflict with her previous and familiar social environment so that,

> It's really frustrating round here where I'm working temporarily in the pub. I have completely different opinions from everyone around me.

In this respect Janice was similar to Jean, another working-class but older modular degree student, who declared,

> I've become much more left-wing than I was before.

This was instanced by her

agonising over sending my son to grammar school which I probably wouldn't have bothered about before.

Like Janice, Jean attributed this politicisation to the historical dimension that had been a part of the social science and English Literature modules she had chosen. She also emphasised the appeal of flexibility:

You can change; that's what's nice about it.

Her first years too had been 'a bit of a mess', but that was because

one of the lecturers left and they never replaced her... Then in the second year it became more like sociology – a lot of statistics and less of interpersonal relationships, and the lecturers were not so good, so it was a bit disappointing. That's only that subject but the English literature was wonderful all the way through, which is why I stuck to it.

Womens' studies, which was Jean's third subject,

was very unusual. The woman who did it was very intent on making us aware how women are oppressed by the way men have been treating them for hundreds of years, but then, when it came to the essays and exams, we had to do them in the traditional way that men have been doing it for hundreds of years, so she was a bit of a contradiction. She was very encouraging and helpful on a personal level. I found that overall, most of them [the staff] were like that – very good. There were no men on the course. They weren't allowed. She wouldn't have them. I suppose she wanted to encourage us to be revelatory but it didn't happen because she was a bit intimidatory. [By contrast,] in literature we all talked and joined in the discussion.

Nevertheless, Jean found women's studies rewarding:

Oh yes, not half! Because another thing I did on women's studies was women's art and I went to interview Paula Rego and I did another project about Gwen John which I found really interesting. The lecturer was really good for that, excellent.

On the course as a whole,

I think it's taught me how to write better,

which, since she aspired to become a playwright, was the point of the exercise,

how to be more economical with writing and less subjective.

But also,

Meeting all these other people, it's also shown me different ways of life.

Helen, another mature, working-class student, went into the modular degree scheme in order to teach, and so in the first year when

> you pick from a whole range of subjects, I was advised the sort of things to go for as a prospective teacher and we've just covered so much ground it's been really good... because with a modular degree you're constantly assessed so you're very aware of what is wanted by the tutors so hopefully you're building all the time and going in the right direction and I think if you haven't got there by the third year they let you know.

Grace, by contrast, had used the flexibility of the modular degree to combine two subjects – a BSc in new technology and a BA in art history. This was 'frustrating':

> because I think if you're doing two separate subjects, two separate disciplines, sometimes you find yourself drawn towards one more than the other and they expect you to do as well as the single degree students. My survival was just learning to forget about competing with the single honours students and be non-competitive and just get to more or less understand the subjects.

Revealingly,

> You have a sense of them as different disciplines because the kind of knowledge is different but the thinking processes become the same. Perhaps you write differently for an arts subject in your exam for instance.

The interviews with the modular degree students revealed many of the familiar problems of running such programmes of study. Janice, for instance, complained that her choice of modules had been constrained by timetable availability.

> This year I did science – well it was about the social consequences of science – and politics which was the only thing that fitted into the timetable. Sometimes it ends up like that; you fill in all the forms telling them what you want to do. You can change your mind in the first three weeks if your timetable is compatible and you don't like the subject but sometimes it doesn't work out and you just have to take whatever's left. That's why I went to Middletown Poly.

As Janice explained it,

There is a special deal between Inner City and Middletown so that anyone at one place can study at any other.

This did not seem to interfere with the institutional identity of students, as it has been seen was a fear of some 'hardline' staff interviewed at Home Counties, even though Janice reported,

Some people changed completely from one place to the other.

This process was however reciprocal, so that it appeared that Inner City gained as many students as it lost. The main inhibitions to such transfers were practical:

Over there they have semester courses [which at that time Inner City did not] so all my subjects were really messed up, but it worked out alright because politics and science were really interesting but Christmas really was a nightmare: I was working like a madwoman, doing about eight essays at once and then I took the South East Asian studies exam in January and got that out of the way. I don't think you learn enough in that time [one semester]. A lot of people failed.

Similarly Jean complained that

The modular degree sort of opened up too many avenues really 'cos you kept finding things that you wanted to go off and read about but there wasn't time... Another thing that is not so good about it is that you don't get really thoroughly involved with one group of people, which is not so good for everybody. And also we did tend to find, especially with the psycho-social studies, you were almost a second-class student, not a proper sociologist or psychologist – there was a slight feeling of left-outness. They tried not to do it but you did feel a bit left out and it happened in other departments as well, like history, where a friend of mine was. Then we had one thing that made me really angry about the cultural studies element of our course: they had trouble time-tabling it and the lecturer would only teach it when the cultural studies students could go and we couldn't go 'cos we had lectures at other times, so we never did that unit. The other thing that wasn't very good really was the muddle at the beginning of every year – you'd go along and look at the timetable and find that you couldn't follow the courses that you wanted to do, even if you were following them through from the year before. We were invited to make comments and everybody mentioned that. We found that we were doing more work than the full-time students because the lecturers for each unit think that their unit is the most important and they forget that you've got five others to do as well.

These complaints seem to be common to the implementation of modular courses elsewhere. However, they can be overcome by good organisation and by counselling and guidance for students through the system, although this takes time, and extra resources are needed. On the old modular degree at Inner City, as Helen mentioned,

> The tutors are always available and always very open. They were there if you needed them. You have a year tutor and another one but to be honest I'm not a one for tutorials; I'd just go to them when I had an essay to give in. There were other students who were there before, after and during assignments. The seminars were when we all met up. We didn't have them in the first year but we did them more in the second year and then a lot in the last year, which is a good thing to sort of phase them in because you develop your confidence. We all dreaded them but I think they were very good for you, getting up and talking in public. It could be very different depending on the size of the group; like in linguistics there were two sets, one on language and the community and the other on learning a second language, and in that set there were only five of us.

Like other students interviewed at Inner City, all these modular degree interviewees mentioned, in addition to such 'personal and transferable skills' of presentation as above, the acquisition of computing and word processing competences, since these had also been compulsory elements of their courses. In addition, Helen had 'learnt a bit of French along the way'. As she explained,

> You have the opportunity in the second year to do a first year set so I decided it would be a good thing to build on the French which I had from school but as it turned out it was a very useful thing to be learning a second language whilst at the same time studying the acquisition of a second language in linguistics. I became very critical of the way my tutors were teaching French, well not all of them – only some!

In this way, one module could be combined to complement and illuminate study in another.

The interviews with Inner City students on what was then the modular degree course have illustrated some of the common practical problems of implementing such course organisation. They also show that neither loss of informational content nor general level cognitive knowledge need necessarily accompany the transition from traditional specialised academic degree courses to modular structures, as a means of moving from elite to mass higher education. There is, however, a tendency for there to be a loss of content, both at the level of specific information, and as higher level, general knowledge and skills. This was shown by our example of the modularised engineering degree in the previous chapter (see p. 109). On the other hand, there is a counter tendency, shown in Jean's complaint above, for modules to become overloaded – with information at least – as lecturers attempt to cram them with the essentials of their special subject as they see it.

Effects of modularisation on staff

In either modularised or traditional academic curricula, the critical feature for student learning remained the enthusiasm of the individual teacher for the subject being taught (though, particularly in modularised, but also in traditional courses, such enthusiasm could lead to overloading). The determination to learn of a self-motivated Independent Study student might carry them through, though even – or especially – then, support from personal tutors has been seen often to be vital. But the crucial factor for most students – as corroborated by all the research evidence – remained the interest in the subject communicated by individual teachers. Our student interviews confirmed this high opinion of lecturers who communicated interest in their subject, as opposed to interest in their research – usually of only limited interest to undergraduate students. If teachers were interested themselves they could invariably interest their students. (To this rule, as to any, there are exceptions – sometimes eminent ones – tongue-tied philosophers who loathed teaching but attracted students, like Wittgenstein for example.)

Like teachers at any level therefore a science lecturer reported,

> You need enthusiasm. You can't do it if you come in of a morning and think "Oh no, not biochemistry again". You've got to be enthusiastic, to keep up with things and point students towards the latest publication in *Nature* and so on. I mean today, I put a slide up and I thought, 'Wow! What a beautiful design of a molecule!' and some people may pick up on that and others may think you're potty but so what? So I think if you lose that you ought to be doing something else.'

Enthusiasm for most academics is maintained through their research interests. Research is however being increasingly concentrated in specialist research centres, forcing academics into a choice between being 'teachers' or 'researchers'. This is a choice they are reluctant to make because many find that their teaching is a necessary stimulant for their research because students always make you rethink what you are teaching. Ghettos of research excellence would indeed predictably produce obscure erudition as academic researchers would tend to follow their own bent towards finding out more and more about less and less. Alternatively, applied research for which funding might more easily be found tends to follow the short-term demands of the commercial marketplace, without allowing time for basic research, fundamental thought and speculative creation and experiment.

But the time they were able to devote to their research was just one of the things that many staff interviewees who had traditionally combined the two activities felt was threatened by modularisation and its accompanying credit accumulation and transfer. They could not even find compensations in the interest that many of them expressed in 'students as people', when they were expected and forced to treat students as numbers, and their contact time with individuals was reduced by the constant repetition of short modules.

Dissolution of their subject specialisation into wider inter-relations with other subjects also sapped the justification of specialised research, and meant that discipline boundaries dissolved, facing staff with students who, coming from other subject areas, might have different ways of looking at things. The hierarchy of teacher and taught was thus undermined and control lost over induction into particular disciplines.

Modular reorganisation however threatened academics not only with the loss of their research, to reduction to the level of mere teacher but also, when students are expected to teach themselves, to the level of coordinator and 'facilitator' – a purely administrative and technical function. The accumulation and transfer of credit for modules selected from previously separated disciplines upsets not only intellectual but also institutional order. Despite being given devolved budgets as 'cost centres', departments and faculties no longer control their own courses. Instead, institution-wide policies have to be introduced to co-ordinate and police them. A core of administrators manages this process, together with ancillary activities such as offering advice and counselling to students, time-tabling to ensure the widest possible number of combinations, and quality-control to maintain consistency across their assessment.

With further rationalisation the whole mutually transferable modular system could be regularised on a national basis, like the National Vocational Qualifications, following a 'National' Curriculum raised from the schools up into further and higher education. Thus control would be lost even at the institutional level and, with increasing delivery of modules of study by distance learning, particularly using interactive computer aided learning, education institutions of all sorts could become mere 'learning centres' delivering individually customised packages of materials to students following personal programmes of study at home or at work. Such indeed is one version of the place of education in the learning society of the future we discuss in the following chapter.

For academics today modular systems represent a mass-production (or fordist) organisation of the curriculum in place of the pre-fordist, semi-feudal apprenticeship into traditional disciplines of the past. As in contemporary reorganisations of private industry and commerce, but increasingly also in the remaining and semi-privatised public sector, a core of regularly employed managers undertakes the central bureaucratic functions of organisation. Around them a periphery of irregularly employed, part-time teachers fills in with the requisite modules as dictated by student demand for them. (Ironically, these new, 'flattened hierarchies' are presented by management theorists as supposedly post-Fordist organisations.) Such arrangements are already becoming common in the higher as well as the further education colleges.

They are justified as being in the interests of the students, and are supported by many of those staff whom we have identified as subscribing to a 'soft' or service ideal of higher education, in alliance, as we have also said, with the vocationalising policies of the Department of Employment. They are opposed by 'hard' line staff supporting the ideal of traditional excellence and the academic identities which it sustains. Such staff allege that beneath the rhetoric of response to student demand, student-centredness and empowerment of students as clients or customers, the introduction of modules and credit accumulation is in reality a means for management to intensify and control academic labour. Yet these 'hardliners' also, supported by research funding and many of the policies of the rival Department for Education, find themselves reliant upon the market in students to elevate their traditionally organised courses and institutions in the academic marketplace.

The market too is supposed to play a key role in the information society of the future, which the government has committed itself to creating, and of which its further and higher education policies are an integral part. It is time to examine this notion before posing an alternative ideal of what would be a real learning society and suggesting the role in creating it that could be played by education at all levels.

5

Towards a Learning Society?

Rhetoric and reality

Believe it or not, the Conservative government at the beginning of the 1990s proposed to turn Britain into 'a learning society' by the year 2000. For the government endorsed the objectives of the National Education and Training Targets for Foundation and Lifetime Learning which were first formulated by the Confederation of British Industry in 1991. These proposed to create a learning society through a process of 'skills revolution'. This would principally be a cultural revolution, creating 'a new training culture' in which individuals would be empowered with 'real buying power' for career mobility and needs satisfaction. It would involve a partnership between higher education, industry and government, in the words of the 1993 White Paper on Science, Engineering and Technology, 'to harness the knowledge and insights of all three partners to mutual advantage by encouraging and easing the increased exchange and flow of people, knowledge and ideas'.

These were the objects too of the government's 1988 education reforms, which were similarly calculated to motivate parents and pupils or students to achieve higher standards through a competitive market in schools, further and higher education. The market also requires information so that consumers – whether students, their parents or their potential employers – can make informed choices between the competing learning services offered in the education and training market place. The National Education and Training Targets that the new system is intended to meet are expressed in a new framework of National Vocational Qualifications that will be equivalent to European Union qualifications. Together these approaches will, it is intended, create a system of 'ladders and bridges' whereby learners can gain academic and vocational qualifications throughout their lives to increase personal opportunity and contribute to wealth generation. However, it is also recognised that most learning – even, or especially, in a learning society – occurs outside formal education and training.

A 'learning society' so defined is a society which systematically increases the skills and knowledge of all its members to exploit technological innovation and so gain a competitive edge for their services in fast-changing global markets. This is supposed to be now necessary because the industrial competitiveness of the UK is widely accepted as being dependent upon a highly skilled work force, able to innovate and to produce goods and services of a high marketable value. In a competitive global market developed countries like Britain can no longer compete with the newly industrialising nations, like those of the Pacific rim – South Korea and Taiwan for example, the so-called Asian tigers – in the mass production of the heavy industrial goods with which Britain once led the world as the first industrialised nation. Now in order to sell it is necessary to produce for specialised and niche markets in high technology goods and services. These require a workforce that is computerate rather than merely functionally literate and numerate, as was needed for the first industrial revolution. At the same time, the rapid pace of technical change demands workers who are flexibly able to adapt to new technology throughout their working lives. The citizens of a learning society would thus exercise an entitlement to lifelong learning and education, and training would no longer be concentrated upon the young but permeate all aspects of social life.

However, whether the UK workforce as a whole is becoming more or less skilled and knowledgeable is debateable. Indeed, the government has often been accused of following a contrary policy. In seeking to attract foreign (chiefly American but also Japanese, Arab and far Eastern) capital looking to invest in assembling and servicing in Britain as a bridgehead to the European heartland, the government has emphasised the virtues of the low wage, deregulated workforce that it has tried to create. Similarly, work reorganisation and 'culture change' are frequently the goals of employer involvement in the education and training programmes that often accompany the introduction of new technology and new methods of working in their organisations.

As a result of these policies, it is arguable that a process of 'skill polarisation' has occurred at work, together with academic differentiation in education. With permanent, structural unemployment, millions of people are relegated to insecure, intermittent and semi-skilled employment if they are lucky. And in education and training, on the one side are those with special educational needs and on programmes requiring participation in training or work experience as a condition of receipt of welfare or unemployment benefits; on the other are those whose pre-existing cultural capital is legitimated by elite higher education. Between these two groups are the mass of students and trainees, adults as well as younger people, whose participation in education and training is often prompted by unemployment. This has implications for the motivation that is widely recognised as crucial to learning.

So the rhetoric of the 'learning society' does not match the reality of the situation on the ground. Yet even at the level of rhetoric, the tremendous increase in learning required for a labour process based on the conscious involvement of all employees, together with a society of citizens active in their working and democratic lives, has hardly begun to be acknowledged. Only poets and science fiction writers have imagined what a learning society would look like and how it would differ from today's world. Long before the advent of computers, which provide most such speculations with their technical infrastructure, Hugh MacDiarmid, for example, imagined 'Glasgow 1960' in a poem written some years earlier. External appearances of the city had not changed – 'Buses and trams all labelled "To Ibrox"/ Swung past packed tight' – however, the people were not going to a football match, but to listen to a debate on the conservation of energy – 'Between Professor MacFadyen and a Spainish pairty' – while the headlines on the evening papers screamed, 'Special! Turkish Poet's Abstruse New Song./ Scottish Authors' Opinions' – and, 'holy snakes,/ I saw the edition sell like hot cakes.'

Whether the popular culture of a learning society would be as relentlessly highbrow as MacDiarmid imagined, for most people who endorse the general rhetoric of a learning society, education and training are felt to be self-evidently good things, but we have suggested that in many instances they are substituted for more fundamental economic and structural reforms. For the CBI, their proposed 'skills revolution' is part of the modernisation necessary for British industry to compete in high-value, high-skill global markets. For the government, education and training (learning) is also connected to competitiveness, to creating a flexible workforce of highly motivated individuals. There are also the wider aims of 'enhancing the quality of life' for as many people as possible, boosting service sector consumption while preserving 'civilised values' and extending the national culture. A society of 'active citizens' is also widely seen as more democratic and 'responsible'.

Similarly, to be a 'learning organisation', 'Investing in People' – as many CBI-approved companies now style themselves – does not just mean more training; the entire organisational culture would have to change. This cannot be achieved in isolation, especially if the broader society remains inimical to learning. Individuals require confidence in their ability to undertake life-long learning and adapt to new technologies. Such confidence cannot be created by exhortation alone. Nor can people be forced to learn, though they can be forced to work. The key for research therefore is to identify and for policy to overcome the economic, educational and social barriers to achieving a learning society in which individuals share high level general knowledge and skill they can apply in different occupations throughout their lives.

Certainly, an integrated further, higher and adult education and training system has a pivotal role to play in a real learning society. In the new system as it is today, further education is already in a vital position between compulsory school education and post-compulsory or continuing education and training. This has been recognised by government in the 'special new emphasis' given to further education since the 1992 Autumn statement. Yet, despite the relative increase in its funding, the position of further education remains critical, with FE college closures and mergers threatened as a result of the competition for students between what are now independent colleges and sixth form centres.

Moreover, further and higher education is still seen as remote by many young people. Typically, the majority who feel they have 'failed' in the academic selection of a minority are discouraged by their school experience from attempting any further study. While the minority who have succeeded feel that they have nothing more to learn. Many adults also lack opportunities for learning in or out of employment. Individual motivation is allied to personal development and economic need in the context of broader culturally-defined structures of employment, promotion opportunities, pay incentives and new methods of work. All these would have to change in a real skills revolution to create a true learning society.

Another critical question facing education and training policy is what knowledge and skills need to be prioritised for the future learning society, and the extent to which concentration on basic literacy and numeracy can be linked to more general, higher-level cognitive skills of reasoning and scientific/logical thinking, by qualifications systems that allow of credit accumulation and transfer. So-called 'personal and transferable skills' are also relevant as they are the core competences required in the many employments that are becoming increasingly similar due to similar applications of new technology and similar reorganisations of work. However, the academic 'national' curriculum in schools is not necessarily contiguous with the more vocational content of much post-compulsory learning. A symbolic and practical division also persists between FE and HE.

Yet, the impact of technological change potentially revolutionises both levels of learning and the methods of its delivery. New modes of delivery, including distance and open learning, pose particular pedagogic challenges to both learners and teachers. As does widening their view of educational settings, and recognising the importance of the workplace and the community in the social mediation of learning, to create a continuity of education and training in formal and informal settings.

There is as yet little evidence that the rapid series of changes in education and training that have taken place in recent years are underpinned by a coherent strategy, informed and monitored by rigorous analysis and research. There remains also considerable uncertainty about the benefits of education and training to the various parties involved. For some individuals it is quite rational not to enter Youth Training schemes, for instance, because they can actually depress their chances of finding waged work. And many employers simply do not require much labour that is highly qualified and certificated. This balance between public and private reward varies across commercial and industrial sectors, and in the relationship of corporate to national competitiveness. There are also market failures evident in persistent 'skill shortages' and employee 'poaching' by employers.

All this gives considerable room for scepticism regarding the government and industry's declared aims of achieving what they call a 'learning society'. Is such a thing possible? Are not all societies learning societies? Or is our society in particular rapidly becoming not more 'learned' but more ignorant?! A glance at the day's domestic news reported by the mass media must give one grounds for doubt – as must, very often, the popular press and television that report them! To consider what a real learning society might involve requires a more rigorous approach. This is provided by what is variously called systems, information or control theory, or cybernetics.

Learning and information theory

To begin with, a society is not necessarily learning just because of an increase in the amount of circulating information and in the means of distributing and presenting it. There is, as we have seen, information that may or may not be integrated as knowledge. There are also competencies and at another level there are skills. At another level again, there may also be wisdom. Information, facts, or data are nothing by themselves, although even to be considered as items for analysis they have been isolated and selected in some way. They are of value however, only by virtue of the meanings attached to them through the (pre)conceptions into which they are made to fit.

Information theory views all thermodynamic systems – physical, biological and social – as involving exchanges of information. Mechanical systems too can be seen in this way, and with the development of automatic control of machines a theory of engineering control has been developed to explain how to incorporate human purposes into machines. The basic distinction of this control theory is that between open and closed systems.

Closed systems are self contained. The machine is set to perform a certain task, primed or fuelled to do so and, as long as nothing intervenes to upset the conditions of its operation, will execute it with perfect certainty of result. A closed system can however be opened to allow of self-correction by the machine so that if conditions change – if it gets too hot or too cold, for instance, or the machine goes too fast or too slow – a servo-mechanism with some sort of sensor to receive information from outside (like a thermostat or a 'fly-ball governor') can alter the machine's activity to keep it on its original course to complete the task it was set.

This opens the original closed system to a new and more open level of determination, one which encloses and determines the initial, more limited system of operation. A mechanical system can be regarded as an analogy or metaphor for describing more complicated systems. For whether these are physical, biological or social, these often vastly more complex and intricate systems can be viewed as exchanging information or energy (which are here regarded as synonymous) to sustain themselves. The simpler systems are open to control by the larger systems that contain them by supplying the conditions (energy or information) necessary for their continued operation, survival or reproduction. No system is completely open however; there are always larger systems of which they are a part up to the universal set.

Information structures in the case of living systems (at least on the planet earth!) give form to cells, organs, bodies, societies and species. The circulating information exchanged with the system's environment that contains or encloses it maintains its structure. That structure or organisation depends upon the finality or purpose of the system, for that is what determines the circulating information.

In this context, individual human needs are defined in terms of sustaining the necessary conditions for the proper functioning of the individual physical and psychic system. If they are not met the behaviour of the individual as system is disturbed. However, human beings are unique in not only being informed by but in forming their own environment through the use of tools. Tools transform objects not only literally but also conceptually; they distance consciousness from its immediate perceptions by forming a new purposive whole of means to end with thought before action. A new and symbolic subsystem is thus created which is capable of self-steering, as it is called in control theory.

Unlike inherited genetic information and animal communication by signalling, symbolic consciousness, and the self-steering system it creates, is capable of learning from past mistakes to act differently in future. Therefore it is an axiom of information or control theory that 'It is a notable property of self-steering that the same state never returns in a self-steering system'.

It cannot be presumed however that the ways-of-life of which individuals as self-steering systems are a part are themselves self-steering, and have not become what information theory describes as closed systems. Such closed systems, unlike open ones, perpetually return to the state from which they started. Like a machine, they complete their operation and revert to rest or repeat it again without variation. Applied to social groups, information theory suggests that hierarchies in power over societies invariably operate solely to preserve their own power by closing systems, to prevent any further development and to lock the social system into repeated identical cycles or loops.

Looking at the capitalist economic system of commodity production as such a closed system, it is clear that the purpose or finality of the system is to produce more and more commodities for sale to rival companies or competitor countries in order to invest the profit that is realised in the sale in the production of more and more commodities and so on in an unending cycle. Whatever the incidental benefits that may accrue to some of the individuals involved in this system of competitive productivism, it is clearly necessary to break out of this particular closed system globally. Otherwise, if we extrapolate from present trends, the human species has set course for destroying the biosphere that sustains it, and which is the ultimate level of its finality or purpose, in that it is the planetary ecology which sustains human and other life and permits its ongoing reproduction.

If auto-destruction is to be avoided, the closed loop of production for profit must be opened to the larger ecological system within which it is contained and which it threatens to disrupt. It is an open question whether the capitalist corporations that now exercise undisputed control over the global economy can adapt themselves to a sustainable environment, for this would mean giving themselves over to a higher finality than the closed loop of production for profit which currently governs their operations. It would mean opening the self-contained and closed subsystem – commodity production for the sake of producing more commodities in order to maximise profits to invest them in the production of more commodities to maximise profits... (recurring) – to integration in a self-sustaining planetary ecology.

Such integration would mean consciously determining precisely how the mass and energy taken from the environment would have to circulate in the planetary ecology, in order to ensure the maintenance of its global organisation, while at the same time ensuring the maintenance of all the individual subsystems which constitute it. This is not a call for the accumulation by a scientific technocracy of supposedly objective information in some vast data base like that planned for the human genome project upon which scientists around the world are currently working. It is a call for the availability of the information necessary for individual members of society to become informed of their own function and purpose at the global level. This information goes beyond that necessary for individuals to be aware of their contribution to the production and sale of commodities or services for the sake of (from their point of view) maintaining and reproducing their own individual and family subsystems through the wages that they earn for their services. Individual and family subsystems are in any case increasingly disrupted by the dysfunctions of the larger economic, social and ecological systems of which they are a part. Closure of information at the level of the individual or family is therefore impossible, however hard we try.

The opening of specialised information systems, which would be necessary to integrate them with the widest possible system within which they are contained, is not compatible with the level of closure of individual enterprises in competition with each other. At this level, individuals' contributions are measured only in relation to the success or failure of their firm, regardless of any other consequences of their actions. Similarly, closure at the level of national economies, or the trading blocks and military alliances of which they are parts, must be opened to the global economy and the ecosphere which sustains them. Thus what is meant by information in a real learning society is not the specialised vocational information which enables the individual to transform inanimate matter, nor the information supplied by manual or conceptual training, but a far more vast scale of information which concerns the importance of the individual as an individual within the human collectivity.

This is a considerably wider definition of information society than usual! It is however connected to conventional definitions by reliance upon the information technology which makes it possible. It also indicates the necessity of preserving and extending social spaces for the creation and elaboration of new ideas. It favours openness to the highest possible level against closure at the level of ideology or dogma. It is also related to the issue of democracy as self-steering.

At present, the triumphalist West has elevated one form of limited representative democracy over every other virtue, save the 'freedom' and 'equality' with which it is coupled. It is doubtful however that the majority rules in any self-styled democracy, beyond deciding between which of two not very different ways to accommodate itself to a global economic system perpetually balanced on the verge of crisis. This metropolitan economy of production for the sake of producing more commodities can only sustain its precarious position by further competition to impoverish the people and degrade the environment of the majority of the world's population.

Now that electronic communications and computing provide new potential for conscious planning and democratic control of self-steering, learning societies, perhaps a new historical opportunity presents itself. The goal however is no longer Utopia but simply survival. As the alternative is posed between survival and destruction, Utopia has become reality. Utopian ideals of a fixed end state of human development, whether as 'communism', 'a free society', or any other 'state of grace', can be forsaken. Instead, we need to develop and implement the collective knowledge of what is required for human survival. New technology affords opportunities to do this by creating an information society in which meaning is given to the actions of individual members of society in relation to their most general finality at the level of planetary survival. New technology also has the potential to inform all citizens as generally as is possible to exercise democratic control towards that agreed common goal.

Telecommunications and computing could then be used not only to considerably reduce bureaucracy, but to increase participation and democracy. There are many possibilities, and local experiments could be started now to discover them and their limitations in the self-governance of as many areas of life as possible – not to mention the possibilities for the reform of an archaic national voting system popularly perceived as corrupt. Educational institutions can provide seedbeds for democracy, as the American educationalist John Dewey proposed, in order to improve the quality of political processes in a democratic society. He suggested that schools and their staff and students should be organised as democratic groups. He also suggested that students should be taught to apply scientific method to problems of concern to their communities. This combination would organise learning in democratic problem solving groups in which students would learn democratic processes and scientific methods at the same time.

As for industrial democracy among those who work but usually exert little control over the use of their labour power, computer-integrated manufacture, which is the logical extension of the computerisation presently being applied piecemeal to production, offers new opportunities to integrate the work of all employees in an enterprise. While requiring fewer operatives (or the same numbers for less time), by storing information centrally CIM ensures that it is communicated to all. The more inputs there are to the system – from designers, engineers, and managers, repairs and maintenance workers, those involved in storage and delivery, sales and marketing staff – the more information is generated and the more effectively it may be integrated for decision-making which may also be computer aided. The logical form of organisation for optimum performance thus becomes co-operative and non-hierarchical.

Information is no longer specialised but generalised, for one part of the manufacturing process cannot act without informing and influencing all the others. As divisions between those who know and those who do, the executive and the rest, are effaced by everyone contributing and sharing information through the computerised communications network, industry can become more responsive to the demands of consumers and to the needs of society.

But new technology extends opportunities for sharing information and decision-making beyond producer associations to the whole society. If information is power then the object must be to share information and generalise power. Power then, like knowledge, no longer exists except as it is shared. The basis for an informed democracy, in which the majority exercise power instead of handing it over to a minority who rule over them, is just that – information and the knowledge and, hopefully, wisdom to use it for the survival of society and humanity.

Education is the single most important investment in the knowledge industry that is supposed to be shifting the economy of the developed world from an industrial to an information base. Education is also, more certainly, the means of generalising information, consciously teaching individuals their place within the largest, planetary set of which they are a part. Its purpose should be to discourage participants from seeing themselves and the purposes of their actions as set at lower levels of finality and determination – just for their own self gratification or that of their family, or the company that employs them, or the real or imagined communities to which they belong, and which should therefore come before all others. Education at all levels must oppose such closed system thinking and help people to develop the conceptual tools to relate the particular to the general.

However, the process of creating a learning society cannot be limited to the schools and colleges alone. The mass media and advertising also have a vital role to play. Indeed, it has been seen that with accelerating social change and to utilise new technology to its fullest potential, education can no longer be restricted to educational institutions but must be recognised as lifelong learning. This is now so generally accepted as to be a cliché, yet its implications have hardly begun to be grasped. We are in a new situation and no one seems to have realised it yet. As a part of the new social situation however, there has been a reaction from the state which is also only dimly apprehended in society as a whole.

The new state we are in

Faced with the possibilities opened up by new technology, there seems to be an instinctive reaction by the state. Dedicated to preserving the existing state of affairs and the power of those who profit directly from the destructive commodity cycle, this reaction takes the form of redoubling obsessive secrecy and closing down and limiting people's educational experiences. Instead of applying communications technology at every level of learning, to allow imagination free reign, to develop from experience the new ideas necessary to comprehend and deal with rapidly changing reality, there seems a desperate rearguard action to push the new conceptions formed from new interconnections back into obsolete subject discipline boxes, as in the so-called 'national' curriculum for state schools. Modelled on the 1903 grammar school curriculum, it goes against the grain of latest scientific discovery. For at present there is a ferment of new scientific knowledge as communications are speeded up and barriers between formerly discrete academic disciplines crumble.

In fact, recent education policy demonstrates very clearly the alternative use to which new technology can be put, to sustain an ignorant rather than an informed society. In the process uncertain and indefinable qualities are being degraded to numerically exact quantities for insertion and sale in the commodity/service for profit cycle. Social goals for education, such as increasing equality and opportunity, have been replaced by the financial accounting of efficiency and value for money. Public services, like education, can then be 'costed' and 'compared' by their users, redefined as 'customers', especially if their infinite and unpredictable possibilities can be contained within narrow enough delimitations of vocationally specific 'outputs'.

In further and higher education the market mechanisms which have been accepted by management typically devolve funding for teaching and research down the established hierarchy from the government's treasury to funding councils to institutions and cost centres within them. As in the other areas of the contracting state, this centralises control in the hands of the funder of the contract whilst making the fund-holder, to whom funding is given, accountable for fulfilling the conditions of the contract. Fund-holders may then subsequently subcontract to subordinate agencies for specific tasks regulated in like manner. At the same time, if the clients of services (in this case students) can be constituted as a market through empowerment by loans, vouchers or credits that they can spend when and where they wish according to the courses on offer, then determination of funding is opened to the market.

As we have seen, the pre-existing hierarchy of universities competing for traditional grant-aided students with a variety of course offerings and residential settings has been extended by the removal of the binary divide and the opening of higher education to larger numbers of mature as well as standard age students, many living locally rather than living away. The courses on offer in the academic marketplace are, as ever, determined by conflicting demands: those of vocational relevance to technical and professional employment; of traditional academic 'quality' which is vocationally irrelevant but related to recruitment for elite management positions; and, increasingly, the demands of the fashionable dictates of what we have called higher education consumerism. In this new further and higher education system students are empowered to choose courses which are regulated by the pattern of their demand – though the market conditions under which they choose can be altered at will by the ultimate funder who contracts for them. An example of this was the sudden and arbitrary government introduction in 1993 of differentiated course fees for arts and science courses in higher education. This threw previous plans for rapid expansion by so many of the universities and colleges into confusion.

Staff who provide the courses must respond to the pattern of student demand. This is especially the case under the conditions of output-related funding already obtaining in further education, where colleges do not get paid until their students complete their courses. But staff also, like fund-holders, set the conditions for the courses they offer on the market. Staff regulate students and students regulate staff, who are in turn contracted to their institutional cost centre, in turn contracted to and therefore controlled by funding councils and ultimately the treasury.

Such a market in education may be new for schools and colleges but it has been replicated throughout the public services. The result is that, as everybody knows, the post-war welfare state is being steadily dismantled. In its place a new semi-privatised public sector is being created that complements the state-subsidisation of the private sector. This is the new mixed economy which has been created alongside the abandonment of the commitment to full employment that was the economic underpinning of the post-war settlement.

The new form of indirect state regulation allows central direction to be concentrated whilst reducing the apparent responsibility of government, and shielding policy from representative channels of accountability. Contract is substituted for representation and charters are substituted for membership. This shifts the responsibility for policy effectiveness off government's shoulders and allows blame for failure to be privatised too. The approach is seen in health with the trust hospitals, in schools with local management and the incorporation of colleges, in the civil service with the 'next step' agencies, in housing with housing associations, and in the area of criminal justice with 'privatised' prisons and the temporarily shelved Sheehey recommendations for the police.

The moves towards a public service market give consumers 'rights', enshrined in legally unenforceable Charters, over the public services they use. These moves have however notably involved a loss of the democratic rights of accountability and public control over the providers of local services – the elected local, district and metropolitan authorities. The latter have been abolished, whilst the former have had their role recast by central government legislation, from being responsible to their local electorates towards becoming boards of managing directors seeking tenders, issuing contracts and monitoring the performance of separate sub-contractors.

The moves towards such so-called 'enabling' local authorities, endorsed by all three main electoral parties, mirrors the 'contracting' or 'franchising' that has occurred in the central state, again with a parallel loss of accountability and democratic control.

There, at the parliamentary level, the vestiges of democratic representation that remain are also becoming commodified, as parties and personalities are packaged and sold in elections increasingly open to media manipulation. Telecommunications used only to provide home-based shopping and distracting entertainments for homebound consumers contribute to this privatisation and consumerisation of social life.

Consumer choice between the range of goods on offer in the marketplace is being confused with democratic determination of what needs to be produced for whom and why, at what cost to its producers and to the environment. Free-market philosophies advocate consumer accountability as the most efficient method of public accountability, substituting 'quality control' for democracy. The logic of this argument, which justifies the marketing of public services, is that a 'free market' is more democratic than any form of democracy. Free markets are thus the essence of and have primacy over democracy, as once stated by Sir Keith Joseph, the grey eminence of Mrs Thatcher's governments. According to such arguments, vast multinational corporations do not need to be made democratically accountable, save to their majority shareholders, for the decisions which they inflict upon, literally, billions of people, because they have been endorsed by the mandate of the market. Local councils, education and health authorities, on the other hand, have to be made 'more accountable' and less democratic, by converting their services into commodities which can be quantified so as to compete in the open market of 'free' consumer choice.

This consumerisation of public life is also a form of modernisation and represents a new sort of 'mixed' economy in which, as former state services are privatised, the state also increasingly subsidises decreasingly profitable private investments. It is the form of modernisation which was chosen, or rather, was fortuitously stumbled upon, by the Thatcher governments of the 1980s. But, instead of affording a way out of the intractable social and cultural malaise that is the legacy of Britain's long decline from industrial primacy and imperial past, this moribund market modernisation leads only to increasing fragmentation between individual consumers and builds upon and heightens existing cultural differences between social groups.

In conditions of pre-existing monopolies, the outcome of competition for what were previously universal services available to all citizens is a two tier health, education, transport, housing, whatever, system. This is daily becoming more apparent, and we have predicted the same outcome in higher education with the emergence of an Ivy League of elite residential and research universities as against the mass of colleges teaching only local and often part-time students.

However, the result of reconstructing the state along the lines of a holding company subcontracting to its component parts is an inherently highly unstable system. Holding companies are known to suffer particular organisational dysfunctions. Managing at arms length a complex range of diverse organisations to which self-management has been devolved brings its own problems. Subcontracting can be a way of reducing the price of a product or service by squeezing the contract, but it typically also involves loss of detailed control, although paradoxically the financial control mechanism is increased.

The relationship between contractor and subcontractor is one of mutual dependency, but another effect is fragmentation, for it is difficult to maintain and enforce national standards or public goods without considerable interference in the activities of the subcontractor. As an example, we have already raised the possibility that a differentiated academic culture will replace the old shared academic culture of generalised knowledge in higher education; we have suggested therefore that the issue of 'quality' is crucial to the new system.

The question also remains as to whether the franchise model of the contract state can neutralise political opposition by privatising the blame for policy failure. The government too, as the ultimate fund-holder, while it may hold all the purse strings and write and rewrite the conditions of the contracts, is left managing a system that is out of its control but follows only the logic of the market. It can therefore feel itself to be, as one former Conservative Chancellor of the Exchequer put it at the time of his resignation, 'in office but not in power'.

For, once established, monetary measures of 'value added' form a closed, apparently concrete and completely self-sufficient loop in a system of reference exclusive of all external considerations. The end result is a new Benthamism in which profit is the only measure of utility, so that, as was said of a previous indictment of such 'Hard Times', 'As the issues are reduced to algebraic formulation they are patently emptied of all real meaning'. Imponderable and uncertain qualities, such as education – the future of which is ever in doubt, because who knows how the ideas of the past will be reinterpreted by the future generations – are reduced to simple certainties that can easily be measured – spelling and elementary maths, for example. Public issues of health and welfare are likewise disguised by the mechanical routines of cost accounting.

The money economy thus intrudes ever more insistently to degrade and devalue even intimate human relations to monetary terms. The individual pays for everything and our freedom from what money can buy is ever more limited. Thus individualism is heightened again and it becomes harder to see things from a wider social or even global perspective, let alone to have any influence upon events. This is a paradox at a time when it is also becoming increasingly obvious to growing numbers of people that the present closed economic cycle of producing more and more commodities for sale cannot continue for much longer without inflicting irreparable damage upon the environment which sustains human life. Thus wider implications impinge ever more insistently at the same time as the commodification of services for sale removes whole areas of human existence from consideration in terms of the larger social and ecological systems of which they form a part. Instead, they are lost in an apparently objective closed economic cycle beyond any judgement of their real worth.

Education is a case in point. It is vital to the transmission of values to the future generations but is by its nature inherently uncertain. It has been degraded more than most public services in the new contracting state. In our schools and colleges the commodification of uncertain qualities is reducing the aims of education to narrowly specified and supposedly objective, quantitative outcomes that can easily be measured and compared. This process is not unconnected, it has been argued, to the growing importance of education in sustaining new forms of class division as the old ones have broken down. Old cultural distinctions rendered increasingly arbitrary by their lack of correspondence with rapidly changing material circumstances can be preserved by the selection of a minority through an antique and academic curriculum. In this case the facility of new technology for reducing cultural qualities to arbitrary quantities can be used to produce elaborate and supposedly objective rank orderings of individuals in a reanimated hierarchy. Then, as has been observed, the more the hierarchical system is staggered and individualised, the greater the sovereignty of the commodity.

This commodification gives rise to a very dangerous way of thinking. We tend to think of other people as objects also, so that they have no other purpose than their purpose for us. This outlook has close links with the idea of ownership. As owners we can do what we like with the objects that we own or that serve us, including – as ultimate proof of ownership – to destroy them. All other wider considerations and moral judgements become invalid. It is a system of thinking closed at the lowest social level of individual desire.

At higher social levels, such as that of state systems, the result of such closed system thinking can give rise to a collective madness. The society is literally mad because it is out of touch with the reality that sustains it. Instead, the atomised individuals who make up the mass of such a society, frustrated in their inability to manipulate others, can find their collective purpose in a false finality.

As Zygmunt Bauman has written in his epochal consideration of 'Modernity and the Holocaust', 'Dehumanisation ... starts at the point when ... objects ... are reduced to a set of quantitative measures ... an entity consisting entirely of measurements and devoid of quality'. This cultural counter-revolution and the accompanying social atomisation of individuals paves the way for a statist reaction, especially as the pre-existing democratic safeguards have been so effectively undermined and destroyed. For as Bauman also says,

> Any impoverishment of grass-root ability to articulate interests and self govern, every assault on social and cultural pluralism and the opportunities of its political expression, every attempt to fence off the untrammelled freedom of the state by a wall of political secrecy, every step towards the weakening of the foundations of political democracy make a social disaster on a Holocaust scale just a little bit more feasible.

That this is no apocalyptic warning is widely appreciated, for who does not share Bauman's recognition that

> the post-modern, consumer-oriented and market-centred condition of most Western societies seems to be founded on the brittle basis of an exceptional economic superiority, which for the time being secures an

inordinately large share of world resources but which is not bound to last forever. One can assume that situations calling for a direct take-over of social management by the state may well happen in some not too far distant future – and then the well-entrenched and well-tested racist and nationalist perspective may again come in handy.

A new social, political and economic compromise is urgently required as an alternative to such an all too predictable future.

Learning to survive

The first priority for any government seriously committed to real modernisation would be to re-establish the central purpose of education, science and the arts in society: to stimulate thought and develop new knowledge and skills to deal with a rapidly changing reality. This would be a real cultural revolution – not the partial 'skills' and 'enterprise' revolutions limited only to vocational preparation and individual competition. Nor would this new learning policy present itself only as learning for leisure. Cultural production is essential, not only for the increased educa-tion and training required for a labour process and a learning society consciously involving all its citizens, but also to encourage the restoration of the environment that the destructive productiv-isms of the past have already gone so far to destroy.

The economic underpinning of such an alternative modernis-ation would be a return to full employment, but not full-time employment. The individual right to work must involve work sharing to reduce hours worked by those in employment, to give them a chance to participate in increased learning at work as well as in cultural consumption out of work (which will increase the market for cultural products and services). Learning at all levels will be integral to such a real cultural revolution but will not be limited to formal education but include recreation, sport and other cultural activities, especially the ecological and community improvement involved in a 'green economy'.

The right to a job in socially useful work must therefore be affirmed at the same time as the right to training, which has been substituted for it – but which is often not training at all; but as well as the right to work with proper training, there should also be the right to learning and recreation of all sorts – the right to earn and the right to learn, as the slogan has it. For training will no longer be differentiated from education and other cultural activities in a real learning society.

The fundamental cultural activity, if society is to be reconstructed from the bottom up, is democratic debate and decision making. Just as we cannot return to the Taylorist productivism of the bureaucratically managed corporate state, so we cannot return to the professional paradigm of the welfare state in which professionals acted on behalf of their clients. The welfare state can only be saved from its present piecemeal destruction by a resolutely decentralised reform in terms of its management and local control, even though its financing will still involve national redistribution according to priority of need.

Aside from the fact that universal nursery education is the single most effective investment in learning at any level that could be made by any government with a serious learning policy, higher education institutions, together with their associated further education colleges, have a vital role to play in the local and regional democratic reconstruction that is now so urgently required. HEIs can provide forums for the public discussion and debate which should in any case be a part of the education of all their students, and which will be the essence of the new social, political and economic compromise that is needed.

Democratic control of universities, colleges and schools, as of other public institutions, must be reasserted by the institution of local (city-wide or regional) democratic structures in place of the accountability through the market which 'free-market' philosophies advocate as the most efficient method of public accountability. The extension of democracy to localities and regions can foster learning and cultural re-creation around the economic and social regeneration of depressed areas. Vocational education must also be rescued from the market place, where it will always be low on employers' priorities. Instead of self-appointed quangos made up of local businessmen (almost invariably) on Training and Enterprise Councils, all public expenditure on education and training must be publicly reported and accounted for directly, to democratically elected bodies.

While the vital role of learning of all sorts in cultural recreation, economic regeneration and democratic reconstruction represents for higher education a reassertion of the service ideal of the polytechnics over the academic ideal of traditional humanism, teachers and lecturers at all levels, together with their students, have to have the academic freedom to pursue pure research at the generalised level that even Mrs Thatcher could see was necessary for scientific and cultural advance (see page 35). But they have to recognise academic research as only one aspect of the advancement of knowledge, and they need to formulate a clearer definition of the purpose and function of academic research and its relation to other types of intellectual activity, particularly those which are taking place outside the universities, not only in industry and business but also, and more importantly, in their local communities and regions.

Academic knowledge and skills must be relevant to the local, regional, national and international communities that sustain them. Explaining their activities to others than their peers could be a good exercise in communication for some academics engaged in more obscure research and scholarship; after all, as the Independent Studies student quoting Einstein said on page 129, 'If an expert cannot explain the basics of his subject to a layman in five minutes, then he is not an expert.'

Participation in learning by as many people as possible is what is required for a democratic modernisation rather than the selection of a professional elite who attempt to monopolise information and knowledge. For generalised knowledge is necessary rather than specific vocational competences, not only to establish the social purposes of modernisation directed towards collective survival rather than competition at the expense of others, but also for the fullest use to be made of the new information technology.

To an extent this is already recognised by those employers who call for more generalised instead of specific skills from their employees. However, we have suggested that employers are unwilling to allow the application of the new skills developed by information technology to render transparent and accessible their own prerogatives of managerial control. Middle managers may be squeezed out, but top employers prefer to sustain the hierarchies in which they are themselves advantageously placed – rather than to apply the technology to its fullest benefit for all, or even for their own firm.

Alternatively, new technology can be used to its best effect in production by charging social and economic processes with information that is accessible to the collective contributions of all involved. Its tendency then is to share knowledge and raise skills generally, multiskilling the majority and empowering them for democratic participation, not merely enabling them to control their personal choice of the commodities presented to them, but generalising power to control the future direction of society and its relations to the world economy and ecology of which it is a part.

The first step to generalising the knowledge upon which to inform democracy and modernisation is to establish for as many people as possible the normality and desirability of full-time education to 18, with recurring returns to learning full- and part-time thereafter. The normality of leaving general and usually full-time learning at 18 should also be used to emphasise the assumption of full citizenship rights and responsibilities for all from the age of 18, not at 25 for some, as has come to be increasingly the case.

All young people have to be brought in from the margins of society, instead of relegating a section of them to a secondary labour market in the regions and inner cities. For those who have been alienated by their previous schooling in an academic and competitive system, the opportunities afforded them by a further two years in college may have to have as little resemblance as possible to that previous schooling, that in any case will have to change, doing away with the outdated and academic 'national' curriculum and its associated competitive tests and league tables. Above all, adequate financial support should be available to students from the age of 16 onwards in order to raise participation rates and the rate of return post-18.

Student loans must be abolished as this only deters the many people who are unwilling to become indebted from entering HE. Adequate maintenance is required so that students have time to pursue their studies and do not have to work their way through college unless they wish to work and study part-time, for which option more allowances have also to be made. Access courses should be extended and people's prior experiences recognised as entitling them to pursue their cultural and intellectual interests, whether or not these are related to their employment or 'the demands of the economy'.

The recommendation of the 1963 Robbins Report, of access to HE for all who can benefit from it, must be reaffirmed. Nor should the definition of ability to benefit be dictated by arbitrarily rising academic entry standards. Higher education must be increasingly opened to all who wish as of right to enter their local college, whatever their previous qualifications or lack of them, full- or part-time, in or out of paid employment. Vouchers, which serve only to subsidise private education and training in the market-place in which they enjoy an unfair advantage, are not necessary to enforce this entitlement, which should be constitutionally and legally enforceable – unlike the empty assurances of consumer 'Charters'.

If the right of all school leavers to enter their local college is guaranteed, progression from schools and adult education will facilitate access to higher education. For those in and out of employment, tertiary/further/adult colleges are well placed to become the linch-pin of the new system of education and training. Before the government cut loose into the market place further education, tertiary and sixth form colleges, making planning and co-ordination difficult if not impossible, FE colleges in particular were well integrated with what remained of skill training in local labour markets and with their local secondary and special schools. They also increasingly franchise the lower levels of higher education courses from the institutions with which they are linked.

Rather than shorten degree courses as the government now proposes, the two years which many already spend in FE before moving on to higher education can become the basis for a new two-plus-two year degree structure. The first two years to 18 for standard age entrants would lead to a broad-based diploma or baccalaureate embracing both academic and vocational – or general and specific – skills. Proposals for such a unitary examination to end the division between education and training have already been published by the Institute for Public Policy Research. Subsequently many diplomates would move on, then or later in their lives, to take their study up to degree level with two further years full-time (or its part-time equivalent) in higher education, followed by two years or equivalent postgraduate study to Masters level.

Such a learning entitlement on adequate grant maintenance will be expensive but it is a social priority that is required to raise general level knowledge and skills amongst the population, which is necessary for modernisation of the economy, as well as to adapt to the accelerating pace of historical and even climatic change.

The costs will be lessened by incorporating independent study into the learning programmes of all students, beginning as early as possible by building upon the project work still widely undertaken in primary schools. Instead of 'cramming' for tests which select a minority for entry to the next stage, the methods of learning and assessment associated with GCSE course work before it was restricted by government should be adopted, and made continuous from the schools through to further and higher education. In a complementary motion, the independent scholarship, research and creation of postgraduate learning should be brought down and integrated into all pregraduate courses.

Thus all individual programmes of study in school and college will include some element of independent study, in the sense of original discovery, creation or research with new forms of assessment and self-assessment based upon their work. (At present only art students are assessed exclusively or mainly on their creative efforts.)

Since many students in such a system will be seconded from employment or on behalf of their local communities, these creations and discoveries will return more than was invested in them, for creative artists, scientists or craftworkers (both art and science being crafts) are the only learners who give back more information than was entrusted to them by their learning. As well as the many practical tasks crying out to be undertaken, there are many unsolved theoretical problems in all fields of learning which subject specialists are too busy to resolve but which are comprehensible to students and on which they could cut their teeth.

Investigation, experiment and debate by all students and as many other people as possible is vital today when so many received ideas in the social and natural sciences are open to question. In addition, new technology can be applied at every level of learning to facilitate routine memorisation and allow imagination free reign beyond the immediate necessity to earn a wage and the constraints of production for profit. This space within education for seeding new ideas must be preserved and extended by making scientific research and artistic creation an integral part of the independent study of all students, rather than separating teaching from research as the government now proposes.

Independent and individual study across traditional subject boundaries can be facilitated by the widely proposed and implemented modular systems of certification. As we have seen, these facilitate access through various modes of part-time and distance learning at home and at work, through the recognition of prior experience, and they enable credit accumulation and transfer. They permit entry and exit points, from diploma level, through to the one year certification, and to degree and masters level, which can ease the present long haul to the final degree.

In a modular system however, it is, as has been seen, essential not to lose sight of the divisions between disciplines as well as the inter-relations between them. It is therefore important to distinguish between 'genuine' fields of study and practice corresponding to defined areas of reality on the one hand, and on the other, outdated and arbitrary academic subject divisions, which only hinder thought and dampen discovery. Whilst advances in knowledge often come from the imaginative projection from one frame of reference to another, this is not the same as a 'pick-n-mix' of modules from different areas of study. If subjects of study are chosen only on vocational (i.e. labour market) considerations, there is a loss of theoretical generalised knowledge in favour of specialised knowledge applicable only to occupational tasks not conceptually related to one another. Philosophical discussion, counselling and support is therefore required if the modular method is not to degenerate into irrelevant educational consumerism at one end, with the myopic relevance of narrow vocational goals at the other. Nor should it become a way of just packing in and processing more students, as it already has in some former polytechnics and many longer established universities.

To ensure that other modular qualifications, like the National Vocational Qualifications, while they are employment-related are not employment-led, educational interests must have more influence in the National Council for Vocational Qualifications. Here again democratic accountability and control enters the frame, for the NCVQ should also be linked to Workplace Training Committees, as recommended by the Trades Union Congress. Work-based assessment involving workers in 'skills audits' (as also recommended by the TUC) should be an essential part of the NVQ approach, rather than assessment by outside professional 'experts'. By liaising with the WTCs, further and higher education colleges can co-ordinate the external skill setting and validation needed to maintain national and European standards if skills and knowledge are to be genuinely transferable between occupational sectors and different firms in the same sector throughout the EU.

The resources are available for the investment required if education and training are to play their part in a programme of economic modernisation and social reconstruction. As stated by another semi-retired former-Minister, the last Labour Chancellor, Denis Healey,

> For Britain the first priority must be a massive switch from defence spending to economic reconstruction. Otherwise we cannot hope to repair the damage done in recent years to our economic infrastructure – our roads and railways, our schools and universities.

Such a redirection of resources can prepare the way for a culture of lifelong learning and recurrent access to further, higher and adult learning. The release of facilities in schools and colleges caused by the (temporary) demographic drop in the numbers of teenagers creates opportunities for providing education and training for the 70 per cent of the current workforce who have not acquired any worthwhile vocational qualification, as well as the four million people unemployed. With the 1991 White Paper *Employment and Training for the Twenty-first Century* focused almost exclusively upon young people, the 3.4 million adults enrolled in further and adult education have been virtually abandoned. Once again, the government's free-market dogma negates its vocational training rhetoric, for the economy has been so run down that FE has become the last refuge for much skill training in local labour markets. Yet with investment in the technology, schools and colleges could respond to the gathering pace of technological change which requires a corresponding programme of retraining throughout employees' careers.

The subsidy of private schools through charitable status and the Assisted Places Scheme should be ended, as much to end the white flight and snobbery associated with the majority of them as to redistribute resources more fairly. The close connection of the elite minority of these schools with the antique universities could, it can be suggested, also be severed by turning the Oxbridge colleges into residential adult colleges like Ruskin college, which is at present under threat of closure in Oxford; i.e., instead of squeezing Ruskin out of the University, Ruskinise the whole of Oxford! This would be widely supported by the many adults who would then be given a chance to attend such colleges. It would also nip in the bud the present moves towards setting up a super-league of semi-private elite institutions aiming to preserve their place at the top of the academic tree through marketing archaic and elite courses to those able to pay for them. It would also lay the great axe to the root of the tree of a system run for the selection of an elite. As Eric Robinson wrote in 1968 in his book *The New Polytechnics*,

> This educational conflict can be resolved only by breaking the domination of the whole educational system by universities which are devoted to the academic ideal.

The ending of the binary divide between universities and polytechnics plus colleges would not then result in the widening of the social divisions in higher education, and the creation of the new academic division that we have predicted. Instead of the polytechnics aping the universities, the original polytechnic vision of popular universities could be spread throughout the new unified higher education sector. However, it is not so much polytechnicians who are required nowadays as polyconceptualists.

These are all practical proposals which could be implemented now to begin to move towards the learning society that will be required in the future. Yet a redirection of resources to enable schools and colleges to provide all their students (as well as adults returning to and retraining for work) with the generalised knowledge necessary for full participation in a modernised and information-based economy would still only provide the technical potential to create a new and unified system of education for work. A new curriculum which facilitates, rather than prevents, transfer between its different levels is also required.

Simply, education can no longer be about selection for the employment hierarchy. We can learn from work but not necessarily just to work. The 'demands' of industry have to be set in a wider framework of human cultural and environmental need. To do this requires a greater contribution of generalised knowledge to work-related education and training. In particular, it requires theory to be related to the specific life experiences of students and trainees – 'work experience' in a deeper sense than it is habitually used. From this standpoint a progressive curriculum must lead on to an understanding of the organisation of the economy as a whole, and of the relationships of power and oppression that are involved in it. Such a curriculum will insist upon international connections, on understanding 'domestic' as well as paid employment, and on opening for consideration the finality of social actions in relation to the larger political and ecological systems of which they are a part.

In a modernising economy, education and training must raise the skills of all workers from the bottom up, much as campaigns in the Third World have aimed to raise literacy and numeracy rates. Education and training combined in lifelong learning will then integrate rather than separate manual and mental labour. If education is to build the skills and knowledge base of society to take fullest advantage of the latest developments in technology, it must begin by recognising how new technology has been applied during the economic restructuring of the last decade, to deskill many of the tasks involved in production, distribution and services. Resources will have to be specifically targeted at the poorest localities to overcome the disadvantage resulting from this process, reversing present priorities. New technology can now provide the potential to enable all working people to become multiskilled and flexible in a true sense, able to undertake a wide range of specific and general tasks, including self-management of their cooperative enterprises and democratic government of their society.

In terms of knowledge and skills, the rapid diffusion of new technology throughout society, whilst obviating previously specialised crafts, expert professions and academic disciplines, also provides the catalyst for the majority of people to begin to think again in a generalised way about social questions. For not only are the latest applications of new technology part of the unprecedented acceleration of social change, which of itself stimulates thought and loosens the hold upon a changing reality of old mental paradigms, but new technology also presents information in new forms, and breaks down the old barriers between previously discrete bodies of information.

However, for information to be transformed, by the unique human capacity to envisage alternative futures, into the knowledge that action is necessary now to avert destruction in the near future requires a combination of widened access to information technology with the democratic forms necessary to act upon the information acquired. Only information combined with democracy can provide the knowledge and skills necessary for survival.

Unlike other species and previous civilisations we do not lack the information to predict nor the means to redirect the course of our society. The real question is then whether humanity can exercise its unique capacity to envision the future in order to open its present closed system to a level beyond its own self-destructive perpetuation.

The only historical precedent for the current challenge presented to human survival are those that faced society in the last national emergency during the second world war. This time however no nation can hope to meet the challenge alone; and within countries alliance on terms of equality, co-operation and planning will be required, now as then, merely to survive. With education at all levels returned to the democratic control of their localities and regions, this would serve to generalise science and raise awareness of the radical transformations required to avoid ecological catastrophe, through a real modernisation of the economy and society.

All this challenges the existing hierarchy in society between those who think and those who do. Such a prospect, of overcoming the division in the working population between intellectual and manual labour, widening genuine access to all and allowing direct democratic control of a unified vocational education system by the people it serves, is daily becoming more necessary, if education and training are to contribute to, instead of hindering, human survival. Beyond individual freedom within all its limitations, free societies might then find new collective purpose in giving themselves over to securing the survival of the species.

Conclusion:
Higher Education for a
Learning Society

Such visionary possibilities as those outlined in the last chapter may be all very well, but such grand plans depend for their realisation on political forces that do not yet exist. So what are the staff and students of the new higher education to do now in the situation as they find it?

Often it seems that as individuals we are powerless to comprehend let alone challenge the situations we find ourselves in. This book argues, however, that there are things that individuals can do together to change the present state of affairs and that they begin with an objective understanding of society, and its development from our subjective position in it. Such an overall comprehension is possible though it is not easy. It can be achieved, for teachers and taught, by integrating into all their learning projects elements of reflective pedagogy, independent study, logical argument, collaborative working and democratic discussion.

We cannot offer a detailed prescription of how this is to be achieved in all educational institutions. Situations vary, and reflective teaching and independent learning can be implemented differently in various places and times. But this perspective can present a sense of direction and a way forward. A clear picture is also required of the social paradigms offered, on the one hand, by the present market modernisation of society and, on the other, by the old social democratic or corporatist order which the dominant market approach has succeeded; we can then chart a new way forward for society as a whole to alternative political compromise, a new economic order nationally and internationally. The changes in education that we advocate are but a part of this wider picture.

Of course, to answer the old chestnut of a social science essay question, education by itself cannot change society. This is because the central mechanism of capitalist society – a labour market of employers and employees – is beyond the control of education. In fact, most educational institutions are under the more or less direct control of the state that maintains them. Nevertheless, education can develop a heightened awareness in students, teaching that which is useful outside schools and colleges, so that students graduate with positive self-images and the knowledge and skills to get along in the world as far as possible, as well as to help to change it. Education can thus contribute towards wider social change, but the space within education which enables it to do this has to be preserved.

No one who works in education at any level today can doubt that that precious space is being squeezed from primary to postgraduate school. On the one hand it is closed by narrowing vocational relevance, and on the other by retreat into vocationally irrelevant but equally narrow, traditional academic subject specialism. Both are on sale in the new market place and the danger is that between them the wider purposes of education are lost. Thus the cultural ground is prepared for the unthinking acceptance of simple solutions to the complex problems facing society and the world today.

Crude reductionism, which imports language and explanations from one level and subject of study, to apply across all levels of explanation, is but the obverse of simple relativism, which abandons any attempt at causal connection or even integration between levels and subjects of study. Examples of reductive thinking that have recently originated in higher education are monetarism in economics and geneticism, which has migrated from biology to sociobiology and psychology. Relativistic nihilism has also reasserted itself in the 'anti-essentialist' fashion for facile intellectual deconstruction, which categorises any attempt at totalising reconstruction as 'totalitarian'. This approach is now so ubiquitous as almost to present itself as the new orthodoxy in the social sciences. Both reductionist and nihilistic approaches are likely to be accentuated by the dismantling of discrete disciplines into under-resourced, unsupported and isolated modules of study.

The crucial question which students and teachers face today is the preservation of the quality of their educational experience, to maintain what we have argued was until recently a unitary academic culture; in other words to prevent the emergence of divergent academic cultures, of generalised and vocational knowledge, which would shadow the already existing, and heightening, social differentiation in the newly reformed hierarchy of competing universities and colleges. It would be ironic but only too typical were this divergence to occur under the nominal unity of the post-binary university and college sector.

Yet in this all too likely scenario an Ivy League of antique and prestigious academic institutions is predictable. They will recruit leavers from private and opted-out schools, who can afford to pay, for a residential cultural apprenticeship to managerial positions in the elite core of the new semi-privatised state and state-subsidised private employing organisations. This elite cultural apprenticeship will build upon and continue their previous schooling in an obscure academic education which will equip them with the generalised knowledge necessary to rule.

Beneath these top ten or so elite universities, the mass of mainly teaching-only universities and colleges will restrict their students to a more or less limited vocational education, that prepares them for intermittent, insecure employment, adapting flexibly to changing employment demands in the periphery of the remaining graduate labour market. This new professional proletariat, selling, contracting and marketing its services in increasingly desperate competition with others, will nevertheless distinguish itself from a permanently unemployed 'underclass' socially stigmatised by their lack of any recognised educational qualifications.

The responses of the majority of academic staff in our interviews at the contrasted institutions increase the likelihood of this predictable outcome. The predominant 'hard' position, of retreating behind a rhetoric of 'standards', to a donnish democracy that asserts its right to research, and to a tacit culture of inexplicitness in the demands made upon students in order to control them, appeared at both institutions in most departments to have won out in the battle for institutional identity. Only the minority retain the 'soft' attitude of explicit service to students and the community, allied with the vocationalising efforts in higher education of the Department for Employment. Traditional liberal humanism seems to have subsumed what was left of the polytechnic ideal, in yet another case of the academic drift that characterises so much of English cultural history. But the academic competition encouraged by the rival and more powerful Department for Education is a cut-throat scramble in which, by definition, only a minority of the already advantaged can ever win.

However, we have welcomed the turn-around in government policy from the training without jobs of the 1970s and early 1980s, when only a minority of the age range continued their schooling beyond 16, while the majority entered Youth Training for make-work schemes and intermittent, semi-skilled peripheral employment. This half-hearted and underfunded attempt to ape the West German 'dual system' has now been replaced by an equally un-enthusiastic and underfunded switch to an imitation of the North American system of mass education to 18-plus. (Although this has been undermined by a partial return to the Germanic model with talk of going back to basic apprenticeships for work and the Dearing Review's reinstatement of a form of tripartitism for schools.) The social demand for further education and training – or at least for more qualifications – cannot be throttled off however, driven as it is by the engine of continuing class reconstruction. And while its opponents allege that this Americanised system only 'cools out' its rejects at a later stage than the early school leaving it replaced, we have suggested that it also affords opportunities for students who might not otherwise have had them to 'drift up' the system. It also offers, we have argued, opportunities for higher education to contribute to cultural change and social regeneration.

To do this now, and to prevent the further fragmentation of a once unitary academic culture of generalised knowledge, it is essential to recall the fundamental purpose of education at all levels which is, basically, to get people thinking. Given the daunting problems threatening the very survival of society and civilisation, few would dispute that more thought by more people is necessary. We obviously cannot any longer rely upon experts and leaders for simple solutions to complex challenges that have to be met by the active involvement and participation of the mass of the population.

The new mass of full- and part-time students, recruited locally through franchising from their associated further education colleges, and including adults in and out of employment, can be encouraged by their teachers to participate in a level of knowledge beyond their previous particularised concerns. This will increase the pressure to exercise their generalised knowledge in generalised power, through the democratic reconstruction and cultural regeneration of society, which is daily becoming more necessary to save the welfare state, modernise the economy and prepare for long-term future survival.

It must be asserted therefore that education is not essentially or even mainly concerned with employment, although some courses at further and higher levels lead to professional qualification, and many students at all levels are often motivated by the need to avoid unemployment. Yet even on the most vocationally specific courses it is possible to combine general with vocational knowledge. This requires a pedagogical approach that begins by examining the situation of students and staff in education and in society, building up from the particular to the general, and facilitating transfer between them via independent study. This approach implies a disregard for academic distinctions between narrow specialisms, which are in any case becoming increasingly interconnected, not only by new communications technology but by the latest scientific discoveries and newest theoretical perspectives, as well as through combined programmes of modular and independent study. This offers opportunities for teaching students to think, not only by sorting information into established categories, but also by questioning those categories to establish their own classifications and orderings of knowledge.

Such a rational pedagogy would soon unmask the pretence of vocational higher education to guarantee secure professional employment for all, through the so-called 'personal and transferable skills' (actually competences) demanded by employers for so many increasingly similar and insecure jobs. It can be taken as a happy coincidence, and an earnest of the new compromise required between remaining productive industry and education as part of culture, that many employers say they now require employees with flexible and adaptable generalised knowledge, in place of the specialised occupational knowledge of the past. But education must go beyond any restriction to vocational competence, to assert its own purpose of enlightening and opening minds to reasoned and logical argument, to scientific method, experiment and discovery, and to cultural creation and recreation.

An important part of the real cultural revolution – as opposed to the Confederation of British Industry's pseudo-'skills revolution' – to which education at all levels might then lead is democratic debate and determination. This, rather than market determination, should form an integral part of all student experience. It would lead to a real empowerment of learners and teachers, rather than the rhetoric of empowerment through consumer choice of modules in the market place. The reality – and limitations – of such 'student empowerment' was shown by the simultaneous moves by government to abolish the only democratic representation that students enjoy through the National Union of Students.

Aside from reintroducing and expanding democratic control over educational institutions by the local communities, cities and regions that they serve, as well as the student and staff communities that constitute them, to introduce elements of democratic debate and determination to all courses is easier said than done. It is, however, a goal which should inform all relations between teachers and taught, and the active, independent and collaborative methods of learning and assessment that are adopted. In addition, some reflection upon the learning and knowledge/skills learnt should be integral to all courses of study. This type of social pedagogy would be very different from the present psychological pedagogies which deal only in individuals without recognising social inequalities. Students would, it is true, acknowledge their individual strengths and weaknesses based upon their past educational experiences and personal biographies, thus 'learning what they already know', but they would see them in the context of a sociology of learning that emphasised the cultural as well as material distinctions between differently advantaged and disadvantaged groups within society.

There would be no end state of final qualification to such a knowledge. For part of the knowledge which education should seek to convey is that all realisation is provisional and contestable, even if attested by the award of various degrees of certification. These would be based upon evidence that will be agreed as indicative by all the parties involved in assessment – students, their peers, examiners and technical and professional bodies, including state agencies. The point has already been made (and not just in this book) that there can be no final degree of knowledge in a learning society.

The opportunities for progression to and from one level of award to another – additional and complementary, or 'higher' in the sense of more inclusive – are not merely a practical requirement of education courses and qualifications today, that allow of credit accumulation and transfer. Nor is this essential element of facility for accumulation and transfer to be built into all courses as simply a matter of equity and entitlement. The matter is more profound than this; it is a question of transcendence. For students to 'Become that which you are', or 'learn what you already know', as the philosopher Nietzsche urged his readers, is not to reach some rest state of the fully developed personality or intellect, as traditional humanism so often put it, in terms of realising all-round potential. It is to recognise, as Nietzsche did, that there is no such thing as an essential essence to be realised, or innate qualities to be certified, by traditional final examination. For, as the poet Blake expressed it in *Jerusalem*, 'The Imagination is not a state; it is the Human existence itself.'

Even for students apprenticed to the few remaining courses that induct them into processes of professional socialisation with distinct occupational identities, identification with their role in employment should not be complete; especially as that role, if not that profession or trade, is likely to change radically during their working life. They will be less effective in their role if they identify with it unreflectively, because to play a role effectively requires a deliberate distanciation from it and a conscious reflection upon it.

This approach is thus part of a practical consideration as well as an aesthetic one of 'manner', 'style' or 'art'. Such aesthetic considerations are not irrelevant to the increasing part that cultural production needs to play in a future in which, despite all the urgent practical tasks crying out to be done, the potential superfluity of material production – at present largely wasted – affords the opportunity for education to play perhaps the predominant part in cultural creation and recreation.

Self-reflection – the examined life, which Socrates said was the only one worth living – is also a fact of human being, contingent upon our use of tools and symbolic language, both of which distance human consciousness from itself and its surroundings. It is what makes us, in Nietzsche's words again, 'an interesting animal', one that stands back from and reflects upon itself and its environment, and so introduces the possibility of consciously changing things. The realisation of this human freedom was what Marx looked forward to in *Capital* when he described a society of individuals '...fit for a variety of labours, ready to face any change in production, and to whom the different social functions that they perform are but so many modes of giving free scope to their own natural and acquired powers'.

We may be far from this situation, but its possibility is one that should not be foreclosed by limiting student experiences to vocational competences, even in terms of the widely applicable so-called 'personal and transferable skills', demanded for employment. The performance indicators currently adopted to demonstrate the acquisition of knowledge and skills make clear the previously obscure demands made by the tacit academic culture of donnish dominion over students; but they should not limit students simply to competent performance or the rote memorisation of information, but must always lead on to the possibility of further freely undertaken transcendence of their present abilities or understandings. This can be achieved by a pedagogic culture that integrates wider considerations into whatever practical or theoretical tasks learners and their teachers undertake together. Such a culture elevates the question of the purpose of their learning activities to a prime consideration, and invites debate about and reflection upon it, at the level of general level 'cognitive' thought or reason.

Purposive general level or logical thinking, which is a skill that can be acquired and practised like any other, itself provides the criterion for its own development and assessment. For, as is generally agreed, 'those who achieve the most consistent results with the least amount of information can be regarded as the most intelligent'. Or, as the psychologist Bartlett put it, the other way around, 'The most intelligent may be those who, with the smallest amount of information (items) produce that for which others need more information'. This can be seen clearly in cases not only of abstract logical inference, but in practical applications to faultfinding and diagnosis. Such intelligence is best developed collectively rather than individually.

This is a definition of intelligence which points to levels of knowledge and skill that enable the handling of information or data, rather than the ability merely to amass or store items of information in vast quantities – on the *Mastermind* model presented by televisual culture. The conscious application of the rules for ordering information also indicates culturally acquired capacities that may remain inexplicit as long as they are regarded as intuitive and innate to 'gifted' individuals. Thus the clarification of the reciprocal requirements of teachers and taught would be a first step towards a more rational pedagogy. This, it has been seen, is commonly occurring as a concomitant of modular programmes of study.

However, the clear statement of outcomes for modules of study should not thereby close down and limit student performance. Independent study negotiated on terms of equality, through contracts between learners and the organisers or facilitators of their learning, offers the opportunity of going beyond this determination to genuinely new and possibly more open and higher levels of learning, discovery and creation.

For it is not for educators to determine the level of closure to which an individual's ideas should be open. We have already said that people cannot be forced to learn, and minds cannot be forcibly prised open. It is up to individual students to determine their own beliefs in the light of the evidence available to them, bringing them 'to the test of sense', as Harvey wrote of his discovery of the circulation of the blood, 'to try whether they be right or wrong.... We ought to approve or reject all things by examination leisurely made.'

Education should however provide students with the conceptual tools and general thinking skills to question received ideas, so that, as with so many of our interviewees, 'You no longer take things at face value'. Thus individual students can subject their own hypotheses, ideas and claims to truth generally, to the relevant criteria, whether of scientific experiment, logical proof, social research or technical practice. They can then defend the conclusions they have arrived at in argument with fellow students, teachers and others. They can therefore acknowledge the point at which their truth claims no longer depend upon proof but are a statement of faith or an admission of prejudice. Nor can they deny that their thought is in some sense ideological, that it is – as well as a more or less adequate conception of the reality with which they are dealing – expressive of an interest in or perspective upon that reality which it represents.

Moreover, the opening or closing of a system of thought and means of ordering the information they have acquired to another level which is accepted as encompassing and determining it, is, as well as an aesthetic, logical or practical choice, also a moral or political decision that may require democratic endorsement as well as rational agreement to find a wider acceptance. Discussion on these decisions and their implications can be encouraged by teachers in collaborative learning with students. Such discussion can be institutionalised through learning contracts between the students and staff of institutions in which the mutually negotiated courses of study will include elements of independent study, based upon real life projects, and requiring research, scholarship, scientific experiment and artistic creation.

The last of these four academic activities is perhaps at present the least characteristic, save in the art and music colleges to which it is intrinsic. But it should not be forgotten that even in the formulation of the most abstract mental operation, as well as in its exercise as skill or its fluent expression as conceptual representation, 'the inarticulate', as Michael Polanyi said, 'always has the last word'. Linguistic ability should not therefore be confused with intelligence for all knowledge is not necessarily propositional in form, as was implied by the 'hard' academics amongst our interviewees. So it is possible to have what the literary critic F.R. Leavis called 'the equivalent in poetry of a philosophical work – to do by strictly poetic means the business of an epistemological and metaphysical inquiry'. This is also possible through the non-literary means of the plastic and expressive arts, including music and dance art of all sorts.

As one of the two fine art lecturers interviewed at Inner City stated,

> There's technical skills and there's conceptual skills. In recent years the latter have come to be more important [in fine art] so that manipulative skills, tactile skills have been played down because of a concern with what art is. There are technical skills still of course, like welding if you want to join two bits of metal together, but there are other skills to do with recognising what you've got when you've done it, and those are conceptual skills, to perceive and see and make sense of it. Values and judgements are going on all the time, especially in this field because if you take the debate out of it there's no art, because art is essentially a communication of debate in the broadest sense.

This last statement could apply to education as a whole and to its communication through the various media to as wide and participative an audience as possible. For meaning and reality are created through culture. They are not discovered but negotiated by individuals, who thus regulate their relations with each other. The recognition of this process and the part played in it by education at all levels can be facilitated by the integration of elements of independent study into all courses for all students, and by the practice of a rational and reflective pedagogy by their teachers. The positive experiences of Independent Study at Inner City University thus offer a way forward for all students in the education of the future.

Bibliography

Ainley, P. (1993) *Class and Skill, Changing Divisions of Labour and Knowledge*, London: Cassell

Ainley, P. (1990) *Training Turns to Enterprise: Vocational Education in the Market Place*, London: the Tufnell Press

Ainley, P., and Corney, M. (1990) *Training for the Future, the rise and fall of the Manpower Services Commission*, London: Cassell

Ashton, D., Maguire, M., and Spilsbury, M. (1990) *Restructuring the Labour Market, The Implications for Youth*, London: Macmillan

Bailey, F. (1977) *Morality and Expediency, The Folklore of Academic Politics*, Oxford: Blackwell

Barnett, R., (1994) *The Limits of Competence*, Milton Keynes: Open University Press

Bartlett, F. (1958) *Thinking, An Experimental and Social Study*, London: Allen and Unwin

Bateson, G. (1978) *Steps To an Ecology of Mind*, London: Paladin

Bauman, Z. (1989) *Modernity and the Holocaust*, New York: Cornell University Press

Becher, T. & Kogan, M. (1992) *Process and Structure in Higher Education*, London: Routledge

Becker, H., *et al.* (1968) *Making the Grade: The Academic Side of College Life*, New York: John Wiley

Bergendal, G. (ed.) (1984) *Knowledge Policies and the Tradition of Higher Education*, Stockholm: Almquist and Wiksell

Bligh, D. (1990) *Higher Education*, London: Cassell

Boddington, S. (1978) *Science and Social Action*, London: Allison and Busby

Bourdieu, P., and Passeron, J. (1979) *The Inheritors, French Students and their Relation to Culture*, trans. R. Nice, Chicago: University of Chicago Press

Cochrane, A. (1993) *Whatever Happened to Local Government?*, Milton Keynes: Open University Press

Coleman, R. (1988) *The Art of Work, An Epitaph to Skill*, London: Pluto Press

Collins, H. (1989) *Artificial Experts, Social Knowledge and Intelligent Machines*, Cambridge, Mass.: MIT Press

Collins, R. (1979) *The Credential Society, an historical sociology of education and stratification*, New York: Academic Press

Cooley, M. (1980) *Architect or Bee? The Human Technology Relationship*, Slough: Langley Technical Services

Dewey, J. (1916) *Democracy and Education*, London: Macmillan

Earwalker, J. (1993) *Helping and Supporting Students, Rethinking the Issues*, Milton Keynes: Open University Press

Evans, C. (1993) *English People, The experience of teaching and learning English in British universities*, Milton Keynes: Open University Press

Finn, D. (1987) *Training Without Jobs, New Deals and Broken Promises*, London: Macmillan

Friere, P. (1985) *The Politics of Education*, New York: Bergin Inc

Gellner, E. (1992) *Postmodernism, Reason and Religion*, London: Routledge

Green, A. (1990) *Education and State Formation, the rise of education systems in England, France and the USA*, London: Macmillan

Halsey, A. (1992) *Decline of Donnish Domination, The British Academic Professions in the Twentieth Century*, Oxford: Clarendon Press

Hillcole Group (1993) *Falling Apart, The coming crisis of Conservative education*, London: the Tufnell Press

Husen, T. (1974) *The Learning Society*, London: Methuen

Hutchins, R. (1968) *The Learning Society*, Harmondsworth: Pelican

Institute for Public Policy Research (1990) *A British Baccalaureate: Ending the Division Between Education and Training*, London: IPPR

Institute for Public Policy Research (1992) *Higher Education, Expansion and Reform*, London: IPPR

Laborit, H. (1977) *Decoding the Human Message*, trans. Boddington, S., and Wilson, A., London: Allison and Busby

Lipietz, A. (1992) *Towards a New Economic Order, Postfordism, Ecology and Democracy*, Cambridge: Polity

Polanyi, M. (1962) 'Tacit Knowing: Its Bearing on Some Problems of Philosophy', *Reviews of Modern Physics* 34, No. 4, pp. 601–16

Ranson, S. (1994) *Towards the Learning Society*, London: Cassell

Robbins, D. (1988) *The Rise of Independent Study, the politics and philosophy of an educational innovation, 1970–87*, Milton Keynes: Open University Press

Robbins, D. (1991) *The Work of Pierre Bourdieu, Recognising Society*, Milton Keynes: Open University Press

Robinson, E. (1968) *The New Polytechnics, the People's Universities*, Harmondsworth: Penguin

Rosenbrock, H. (1990) *Machines with a Purpose, challenging the view that 'in science, man is a machine'*, Oxford: University Press

Salter, B., and Tapper, T. (1994) *The State and Higher Education*, London: Woburn Press

Scott, J. (1991) *Who Rules Britain?*, Cambridge: Polity

Sennet, R., and Cobb, J. (1973) *The Hidden Injuries of Class*, New York: Vintage Books

Smithers, A., and Robinson, P. (1991) *Beyond Compulsory Schooling, A Numerical Picture*, London: Council for Industry and Higher Education

Smithers, A., and Robinson, P. (1993) *Changing Colleges, Further Education in the Marketplace*, London: Council for Industry and Higher Education

Silver, H., and Brennan, J. (1988) *A Liberal Vocationalism*, London: Methuen

Taylor-Gooby, P., and Lawson, R. (1993) *Markets and Managers, New Issues in the Delivery of Welfare*, Milton Keynes: Open University Press

Thomas, K. (1990) *Gender and Subject in Higher Education*, Milton Keynes: Open University Press

Wallace, C., and Jones, G. (1992) *Youth, Family and Citizenship*, Milton Keynes: Open University Press

Zuboff, S. (1988) *In the Age of the Smart Machine, the Future of Work and Power*, Oxford: Heinemann

Index